REWRITING THE NATURE OF EDUCATION, PEDAGOGY AND DIDACTICS

Dr. Ernesto Hashimoto
Rewriting the nature of Education, Pedagogy and Didactics

Published by Spines
ISBN: 979-8-89383-600-4

Rewriting the Nature of Education, Pedagogy and Didactics

Dr. Ernesto Hashimoto

Contents

About the Author

ERNESTO EDMUNDO HASHIMOTO MONCAYO

He is a senior professor at the Pedro Ruiz Gallo National University (UNPRG) - Peru. He has several doctorates in Peru and Spain. He is the author of many books related to the subject, research and the university.

Foreword

We sincerely appreciate the trust of Dr. Ernesto Hashimoto Moncayo in giving us the opportunity to preface his book. This work represents a fundamental contribution in the necessary approach to the clarification of the conceptual apparatus of education and the science that studies it: Pedagogy.

Starting this journey implies adopting an epistemological position. This has been a habit among those people and experts who, honestly and well-intentioned, have dedicated themselves to its foundation, research and teaching from the common recognition of its central meaning and personal and social meaning for human evolution.

In an extremely sensible way, the author, a doctor in Educational Sciences, has proposed to write about these topics. He does it – let us keep this in mind – in a field where there is a relative versatility and interpretative diversity in concepts, approaches and points of view, which undoubtedly constitute sources of real and potential enrichment. But often many of them have been prepared a priori and from a tremendous lack of knowledge of the nature of education, Pedagogy and Didactics. This practice - in the strict sense 'pre-Confucian or 'pre-Socratic', because it does not incorporate the recognition of one's own ignorance - has its roots, as in other scientific fields, in human egocentrism. But not so much in the 'external ego' or of the immature sciences, but rather in the interior or the biased knowledge typical of unlearned researchers who neither understand the nature of science, nor seem to understand or assume its transcendence. Some results, in fact, have had an impact on the training of teachers and students, partly conditioning the epistemological development of Pedagogy. As the author himself points out, "each incorrectly used concept or category can lead to a conceptual and methodological error."

The first chapter argues about the nature of education with an original approach, highlighting its meaning and meaning. Its essence is specified, as well as, in the author's opinion, some erroneous interpretations associated with this human activity. In this sense, the classist, instrumentalist and doctrinaire character and uses of 'education' have been too harmful - and continue to be so. In particular, in the case of those governments, institutions, de facto powers, isms and people who make deliberately indecent (or 'unethical,' as they would say in classical Greece) use of it to achieve their ends, even when is defined and sold as beneficial for people and society. Some of us have made it clear and published, not only that there is nothing further from Pedagogy than indoctrination, but that the true education of conscience is to a large extent educating for deconditioning, and that this quality of the old human being must be overcome, replaced. Already in science and teaching.

Dr. Hashimoto recovers the classification of education into innate and artificial. Regardless of whether one could disagree with this or not, sufficient arguments are provided that indicate that education, in the first instance, is a natural and proper human process, which occurs spontaneously motivated by its own biological and social needs. By explaining your understanding of these two types of education and their common characteristics, a gap is left for further study, in case you share this position regarding the need to link them, so that both contribute to the evolution of the being. Human as the basis and orientation of the development of society.

The approach is very interesting when expressing that "education forms people before it forms human beings", since education, as a systematized process, should be oriented towards the formation of truly human people who, in addition to their constant self-improvement, incorporate as vital imperative the need to contribute to the improvement of everything around you and the future.

A vehement analysis is made of the nature of Pedagogy, which has been classified as science, art, technique, technology, etc. Although the review includes remote, classic and recent contributions, the disparity it reflects clearly denotes the lack of consensus on its condition and object of study, among other reasons because it has been perceived from various criteria and different educational levels. This heterogeneity in the definition of Pedagogy may have been one of the reasons why other sciences – especially psychology, a health science – have taken on, with intrusiveness and without restraint, topics that are not their own, on which their contribution is necessarily less rich, limited and partial. On the other hand, when, due to ignorance or the spurious interests of others, Pedagogy is not considered a science, its relevance, its strength, its social and professional meaning and its epistemological scope are minimized. In this sense, the author provides sufficient arguments about the scientific nature of Pedagogy with his own and original judgments that contribute to the enrichment of this position.

The author returns to Popper, who states that what distinguishes a discipline is not so much its object of study – which can be shared in some issues – but rather the type of problems it helps to solve. In this sense, there is a controversial point because, if one agrees with Popper, one would have to accept with well-founded and sensible limitations the intrusive nature of some sciences, already mentioned. Another very different issue is that the object of study of one science is adopted to a high extent by others.

What would happen if pharmacists, in addition to their subject of study, dedicated themselves to Medicine itself? In this case, not only would the necessary scientific self-discipline lose, society would lose in the long run. And this, with Pedagogy, is already happening. This loss is undoubtedly contributed to by the striking pedagogical delay or general ignorance of Pedagogy and its enormous possibilities in our reference countries. This does not happen at all in those where education has a higher degree of development.

In relation to the classification of sciences into basic and applied, perhaps the very complexity of Pedagogy would require the existence of a third dialectical, synthetic and inclusive category of that duality, in which it could be included. On the other hand, although the author provides pertinent arguments regarding the education-Pedagogy relationship, the richness of his reasons, as well as his scientific originality and honesty, invite us to continue reflecting and clarifying the relationships between Pedagogy and General Didactics.

The author conceptualizes General Didactics as: "A technological discipline that studies the teaching-learning process both in isolation and in its interaction with other educational components, to make it more efficient and quality in its objective of contributing to the formation of the person." Possibly this notion limits its epistemological nature - which in our opinion includes basic and applied research -, minimizes its importance and narrows its functions, by leaving out other areas and perspectives. This observation does not mean - in the opinion of the prologue writers - that General Didactics should be recognized as an independent science, because we understand it as a science within Pedagogy, whose object of study is teaching for training and social and educational improvement. People. Pedagogy, in fact, includes other sciences whose objects of study, within education and teaching, deal with educational policies, international and comparative education, the history of education and teaching, the organization of educational centers. , non-formal education, research and diagnosis methods in education, educational guidance, etc.

To read and better understand the depth and meaning of this book, we understand that it is necessary to do two things: the first is to empty one's own cup of prejudices. The second is to conceptualize it as what it is: a point of view among several, with which the reader, who in turn has his or her own, will dialogue and ideally investigate. To be able to perform these two gestures, adequate scientific training is essential. We understand that this occurs when there is knowledge and when the knowledge one has is simultaneously oriented towards an openness well compensated with doubt. Only in this way is it possible to ask, and only in this way is it possible to wonder. Perhaps science, one of whose imperatives is not to lose sight of itself, does not essentially consist of something else.

Nivia Alvarez Aguilar
PhD in Pedagogy
University Professor
National University of Nuevo León (Mexico)
Agustín de la Herrán Gascón
Doctor in Pedagogy
University Professor
Autonomous University of Madrid

Introduction

The truth is corrupted by both lies and silence.

— Marcus Tullius Cicero

How is it that, although children are so intelligent, most men are so stupid? It must be the fruit of education.

— Alexander Dumas

Humanity has put all its trust in education to achieve higher levels of well-being. However, reality shows unrest, crime, injustice and poverty on scales never seen before. The same thing happens with families; they have the greatest expectations in education as a support to achieve better living conditions. But, they do not always achieve these objectives. When contrasting desire with harsh reality, the following questions arise: Does education have nothing to do with improving human life? Or has education been so poorly conducted that it has not exerted enough weight to contribute to changing things? Or is it that we do not know what education is and how to get to know it?

Surely the first two questions contain some truth. Regarding the first question, the answer is that education is not everything, it is a factor of change, but a fundamental factor of change. The second question is answered by the constant educational reforms developed by national governments, by the permanent protests of society that show discontent with the way education is conducted. Knowing that education has a great specific weight in developing us as individuals and society, what remains is to seek a relevant and appropriate education to achieve national objectives. For this, as in all things, a level of information is required to transform a reality.

But what is education? In what dimensions of education can we intervene? What type of knowledge is needed to be able to intervene? What disciplines study it? These questions will be analyzed in this book. We wish to warn the reader that this work is only a chapter of the doctoral thesis that the author is carrying out for the Autonomous University of Madrid. It is a chapter that contextualizes the central research topic. To a certain extent, this work aims to clarify the nature of education and the ways of studying it through research.

FE González Jiménez and M. Díez Barrabés (2004) wrote: "it seems, however, that what I try to defend supposed an acceptance of a certain invariability of ideas and concepts or ways of doing, nothing could be further from my thinking (p. 39)". Our thinking is just as far from defending established theoretical positions that are part of our training, just for the sake of being considered "consequent." Rather, we accept that the permanent questioning of our "beliefs" is the most appropriate scientific position. As we also criticize the unrestricted and sectarian defense of thoughtlessly accepted dogmas, or being irreverent with any school or current of thought without the corresponding foundations, since that would be typical of a being lacking scientific training.

With the same mental humility, the author of this work intends to participate in the global debate on this important human activity. Accepting a priori that there are no gods in the "educational Olympus," that there are no "pontiffs" who send their dogmas so that simple mortals can repeat in a heavenly chorus what they want to hear. Accepting that there are very few "self-sufficient" people to whom this anecdote that circulates on the Internet applies:

> *Nan-in, a Japanese master of the Meiji period, received a university professor, who came to ask him about Zen.*
>
> *Nan-in served the tea. He filled his visitor's cup and continued pouring it. The professor watched as the cup overflowed, until he could no longer contain himself and shouted:*
>
> *"The cup overflows. "There's no more room!"*
>
> *"Like this cup," Nan-in said, "you brim with your own opinions and speculations. How can I teach him Zen unless I first empty his cup."*

Rather, it is believed in the existence of a healthy mental openness, of a tolerance for other ideas, because "ethnocentrism" is a form of intellectual discrimination, and an obstacle to the development of knowledge. It is also believed that all well-intentioned people with something to say, who live in the east or the west, who study in the north or the south, whether they are known or ignored, with their effort and talent can contribute to the construction of the great educational enterprise, providing its relative truths in the desire to be useful to the world. More than in any other discipline, it is in education where the use of the "force of reason" and not "force as reason" is expected to correct what has to be corrected, modify what has to be modified or changed. Whatever must be changed for her good.

Because each concept or category incorrectly used can lead to conceptual and methodological errors, and this is because concepts are the intellectual tools that people have to understand and act in reality. Concepts reveal the essence of a set of phenomena that are described to understand a complex and diffuse reality. When the researcher does not have sufficient foundations, when he does not have clearly established the meaning of these concepts, his performance will have limitations or will be poor performance. Research, the most important activity in science and technology, is one of the most affected by this phenomenon.

When research is carried out by confusing concepts or working on a vague concept, the ultimate goal of the research is lost in inconsequentiality, in small and sometimes meaningless research. The same thing happens when a research is not located according to its nature. For example, if the nature of a discipline is technological, and the researcher acts as if it were scientific, its results will serve to fill the shelves of a hidden library, since they would have no impact to control and transform their reality (I go back, it would have the impact of harming the training process of new researchers). On the contrary, establishing that the field of action involves scientific work will guide the scientific community to search for these laws and theories so that they can serve as input for technologists, so that they can generate the efficient and effective solutions that are needed to achieve the objectives raised.

It is accepted that encyclopedic, that is, repeating what others have written, can be useful to clarify concepts, but this has its limits, especially in the scientific field, since science is not concerned with preserving knowledge but with renewing it. , if that is necessary. So an intellectual should not doubt and fear what is established, if with the well-founded reflection or the evidence presented, unintentionally, it generates disagreement or refutes the very established positions of certain currents.

Disagreement is normal among intellectuals, and it occurs because we know different things, or because of prejudices (cognitive and emotional) against others, or because of ignorance, but also because of a whim. However, these disagreements, properly carried out, translate into outlining or improving the arguments as the history of science teaches us: for the good, discussions in Biology, P. Lorenzano (2000) tells us about the intellectual confrontation between JC Smart and M. Ruse and R. Munson, about the existence of laws in Biology (this confrontation is not necessarily in the same space and time, since at the same time Smart's proposal in the 1960s, his opponents "answered" him in 1970 and 1975 respectively). Also well-known is the discussion on the "completeness of quantum mechanics between Einstein and Bohr, which was formally held at the Solvay congresses of 1927 and 1930." (A. Dieguéz Lucena 1998, p. 57). But there are also disagreements that are conducted inappropriately, such as that between Galileo and the Catholic Church.

Agreeing with other scientists is useful for building the edifice of science, because it allows this explanatory vein to be enriched through new experiences or arguments, managing to accumulate evidence for scientific discourse. It involves building a scientific community with an "ethos" supported by these laws. But disagreeing with or refuting a theory or law is also beneficial to scientific work, since it can generate a rupture that directs the fact or phenomenon being studied towards other explanatory levels, or profiles the conceptions held about a certain situation or condition, of things.

Some warnings for reading this work: first, the norms, principles or epistemological criteria used are those accepted by the community of epistemologists known in the field of scientific realism, such as M. Bunge, K. Popper, etc., for an epistemology normative, and not the criteria established by descriptive epistemology such as Rorty, who promotes the acceptance of a proposal, based on the consensus of a social group. Second, the concept discipline is used to refer to a set of knowledge accepted by a community that serves to describe an object of study. Third, throughout the document, for each topic, the range of interpretations that have historically been presented is presented, and then the author develops his own version of it.

The first chapter deals with the nature of Education, moving away from the characteristics established in the documentary history and describing other characteristics, which allow us, in our opinion, to complete its real nature. The second chapter is a modest logical and epistemological exercise to establish the nature of Pedagogy, disagreeing with many theoretical positions. The third chapter uses all the theoretical and methodological resources to rewrite the nature of Didactics, its result is very controversial. Although the reader could question what was written, because it is his right and because there are no dogmas in science, what cannot be doubted is that this proposal is made with intellectual honesty, whose only interest is to contribute to the clarification of a discipline so important for The education.

In the last two chapters of this work, it has been written using a strategy, which P. Freire called "the Pedagogy of the question" or what Socrates called "the elicitation." Narrative strategy that allows readers to discover the essential messages of the work in an orderly and precise way. However, the fundamental reason for using this strategy is to honor the wise intellect of P. Freire and Socrates.

With this work, which is a research limited at the metatheoretical level, the aim is to provoke the questioning of what is established, given that one is dissatisfied with the status quo. The aim is to develop an analysis model to better understand Education: the most important social activity of humanity, along with Pedagogy and Didactics. The theoretical and methodological proposal that is proposed follows the spirit of Alstedio, a character from Comenio. "Alstedio adds: Whoever wants to disagree: I propose the path and the motive that I would like all those whom I would like to be highly educated to follow." (Juan Amós Comenio. 1998, p. 114), and also that of KR Popper, when when asked for an explanation, like the one in this work, he said:

If you asked me: How do you know?, my answer would be: I don't know; I'm just proposing a conjecture. If you are interested in my problem, I will be very happy if you criticize my conjecture, and if you present counterproposals, I in turn will criticize them [...], the theory of knowledge advances through conjectures and refutations (KR Popper. 1983, p. 192).

Rewriting the nature of Education, Pedagogy and Didactics, the objective of this work, is a task of high ontological, logical and epistemological content. It is a research circumscribed at the meta-theoretical level. The concern that motivated it was to contribute proposals to the cognitive domain of these disciplines, by providing elements of analysis and reflection not so common in specialized educational literature. Therefore, the enlightened and noble reader is asked to free himself from prejudice, grow in consciousness, to analyze the message without considering who wrote it.We hope that this document, as an educational proposal, fulfills the mission of opening the academic debate. Therefore, well-founded questions and unprejudiced criticism are gladly accepted, so that in the end they translate into concrete actions that help transform education, so that it meets the objectives set for it.If for the keen reader the arguments are unfounded or twisted, then clarifications are requested, so that they can be corrected in this document or another.

The Nature Of Education

What is education? Is there only one way to understand education? What do we mean when we talk about education? Are there different kinds of education? These and other questions will be answered throughout this chapter.

CHAPTER 1
____

NATURE OF EDUCATION

Either we learn education at home or the world teaches it with the whip, and we can hurt ourselves.

— FRANCIS SCOTT FITZGERALD

1.1 Definitions of education.

The nature of education from an etymological point of view is accepted by consensus by almost all scholars. J. Dewey (1998) summarizes it:

Etymologically, the word education means precisely a process of directing or channeling. When we take into account the result of the process we speak of education as a structuring, molding, formative activity, that is, a structuring according to the normative form of social activity (p. 21)

Later he points out:

To say that education is a social function, which ensures the direction and development of immature beings through their participa-

tion in the life of the group to which they belong, is equivalent to saying in effect that education will vary with the quality of life that prevails in the group. (J. Dewey 1998 p. 77).

However, this consensus is lost when attempts are made to place education in certain cultural contexts, due to the multiplicity of perspectives of specialists on education and of the people who make decisions about it. For example, Rufino Blanco (1930) already identified up to 184 definitions of education in 1930. In 1952, T. Díaz Fabelo (1958) systematized 133 definitions. Surely, the number of current definitions has increased significantly.

Following the criteria of the main theories or systems, Paciano Fermoso (1985, pp. 153-170), ordered the following definitions of education (whose position was altered to respect the chronology):

Plato (idealist): "We have said, and with reason, that a good education is what can give the body and soul all the beauty and all the perfection of which they are capable." "Education is the art of attracting and leading young people towards what the law says is in accordance with right reason and what has been declared so by the wise and most experienced elders."

Sto. Thomas (perennialist): "Education is the promotion of offspring to the perfect state of man as man, which is the state of virtue."

Rousseau (naturalist): "Education is the work of nature, of men or of things." "Education is the art of educating children and training men." "Education is nothing but the formation of habits."

Herbart (realist): "Education aims to form character in view of morality." "It is the art of constructing, building and giving the necessary forms."

J. Dewey (experimentalist)*: "Education is the reconstruction of experience that adds to the meaning of experience, and that increases the ability to direct the course of subsequent experience."*

Dilthey (culturalist)*: "By education we understand the planned activity through which adults try to shape the lives of developing beings."*

García Hoz (personalist)*: "Education is the intentional improvement of specifically human powers."*

Peters (logical analyst)*: "Being educated implies mastering certain practices; knowledge and understanding of principles. For this ideal to come true, it is necessary to learn a lot of different things. Consequently, it is logical that we begin to consider the existence of more than one educational process." "The educational processes are: training, instruction and learning through experience, teaching and learning of principles, the transmission of critical thinking, conversation and the 'total man.'*

Following this same criterion, other authors could be added, for example:

G. Kerschensteiner, (1926, p. 15) (neidealist):"Education is a sense of value, of individually determined breadth and depth, elicited by the subject of study and organized differently by each individual" This development of personality is the central task of the educational process. The ultimate objective is "the moral improvement of the community" (1926, page 189)

Herman Horne (neoidealist): "Education in the superior external process of adaptation to God of the physically and mentally developed, free and conscious human being, as manifested in the evolutionary emotional intellectual environment of man" (Taken from George Kneller. 1967, p.35)

Émiledurkheim (1976, p. 98) (structuralist-functionalism):

Education is the action exercised by adult generations on those who are not yet mature for social life; Its objective is to raise and develop in the child a certain number of physical, intellectual and moral states that are required of him by both political society as a whole and the particular environment to which he is specifically destined.".

Pinkbuenfil, Burgos (1992, p. 12-13) (Analysis of Marxism):

For Lenin, education is an instrument of politics, for Althusser, education is an ideological practice; for Gramsci all educational practice is a political practice, for Marx it is a cultural practice. Only in the case of Lenin is there a clear, pragmatic notion: the political and the educational are related in terms of exteriority and subordination. Gramsci and Althusser, despite making evident a political object alongside all educational practice, do not imply the link between the two in instrumental terms. From the relationship between politics and education, it is possible to define what is specific about educational practices: for Gramsci, it is a hegemonic relationship from which those who participate in it appropriately ("feel, know and understand") of a content (forms of "higher" knowledge) that, prior to said relationship, they did not have; For Althusser, it is an ideological practice (interpellation) from which the subject is constituted, that is, he assumes or accepts the traits and characteristics that said interpellation proposes and recognizes himself in them; For Lenin it is a practice subordinated to a political project that consists of the incorporation of "scientific knowledge" and political positions consistent with such project; For Marx, it consists, in a similar way, in the appropriation of knowledge that serves those who are educated, to free themselves from forms of oppression..

ECLAC/ OREALC (1992) (Pragmatism): Education is a privileged instrument for the development of social capital and social cohesion; contributing to improving relationships of reciprocity, trust, tolerance and social integration. It is a development strategy to increase competitiveness and social inclusion; it turns knowledge into a fundamental input of the productive process, making investment in Human Capital more than ever necessary for technological progress, competitiveness and growth.

Even though Paciano Fermoso (1985, p.162) recognized the existence of an excessive number of existing definitions, as is normal for any scholar of a topic, he ventured to provide us with a new definition: "Education is an exclusively human, intentional process. , intercommunicative, and spiritual, by virtue of which the instruction, personalization, socialization and moralization of man are carried out more fully.

All the definitions indicated above summarize education, partly defining its nature. However, up to this point they are exclusively a compilation of authors; below, the nature of education is presented analytically, according to the author's reflection. The concern of this work goes beyond stopping at the characteristics well documented by education experts, such as: socialization, communication, etc., to address characteristics that are little discussed.

1.2 Characteristics of education

Education, as a historical process of society and the individual, goes through two stages: the first stage, which we would call natural or innate education, and the second stage, artificial or mass education. The meaning of "natural education" is not the same as that given by Rousseau, since it refers to the education of the child's senses according to nature and his environment, respecting his natural rate of development. Nor that of Wolfgang Goethe, who in his novel "The Pilgrimages of Wilhelm Meister" describes how children are educated in a very natural way, but said naturalness to educate refers to the respect of teaching them the arts and techniques according to the inclinations and the degree of maturity that each one has. From our conception, natural education has nothing to do with the "natural" capabilities of the child or adult, it refers to the innate act of the human being to provide cognitive and material tools to their offspring so that they live in happiness.

1.2.1 Differences in natural and artificial education.

These two stages of education have certain differences but also some common characteristics.

The first big difference is that natural education is an innate activity of the human being and is motivated by the emotional relationship between the protagonists of the educational process. The innate explained from the biopsychological point of view, referring only to the pre-existence of unlearned skills and behaviors, without referring to the pre-existence of cognitive elements, as postulated by the doctrine of innatism or Fodor's innatism; in natural education The motivation to teach content and values is supported by the instinctive love of the mother or father, or by the natural affection of friends, or by the agape love of religious teachers. In artificial education, there is no obligation to show affection; in many cases, it is impersonal. The task of teaching is professional, following techniques and procedures to make their work more efficient, without weighing their effects on the student's personality.

Natural education in its historical-social beginnings is instinctive and unsystematic, beginning at home and ending in the training of the elderly, seeking to give them the basic cognitive and moral tools so that their children can function successfully in the community (success from the contextual point of view implies: being happy or surviving or adapting to the system). Artificial education from its beginnings was characterized by being systematic and planned.

From the same perspective, Félix E. González Jiménez (2012, p.646) defines education "as the natural continuity of genetics, the most necessary, important, transcendent but insufficient activity of human beings. As far as its natural insufficiency must be permanent." Or as he postulates Giovanni Enrico Pestalozzi, with his premise "life educates," stated in his book "How

Gertrude teaches her children" (1801), where he not only describes the mother as the symbol of the highest educational operator, but also, as in The school originates from his bosom before anyone else's, and his own.

Beyond the scholars' own opinion, it is everyday evidence that shows us that, no one teaches parents how to teach their children and no one teaches their children how to learn. They teach and learn by instinct, because they have it incorporated into their genetic or mental structures. The evidence shows that no one forces or teaches parents and friends to be affectionate towards their own.

To explain the innatism of education and its emotional motivation, we rely on the two aspects that explain the origin of man: creationism and evolutionism.

From the creationist point of view, God created man in his image and likeness. When God created man, God's correct attitude was to teach Adam how to proceed so that he could live happily in paradise, giving him instructions to subjugate material things (animals, fields, etc.), values or principles of life and freedom so that act according to limits set by God himself, for example, not eating from the "tree of good and evil." And if it is true that "God is love," then it was that feeling that "forced" him to educate his creatures.

Since man is his image and likeness, it means that man has incorporated into his nature the teaching of his children, a teaching that begins with love, a divine quality incorporated into the emotional structure of the human being. This divine love was revealed by the Greeks as the affectionate feeling, of desiring good, that a person feels towards their friends, family or unfriendly and unknown people, described as Philía, Storgé and Agape.

This natural teaching of man towards his offspring had to incorporate instructions on mastery of nature, values and principles of life, and freedom with certain limits provided. So from this perspective, the basic functions of this education were: to instruct from love, and to moralize their descendants from the word of

God, so that they live harmoniously on earth, "resembling God." Therefore, the fundamental objective was to achieve the happiness of the person and the well-being of the community through obeying and serving God.

This education involves training man in freedom within the limits of divine laws, constituting an understandable paradox: being free but under the imposition of God or his parents. The Italian pedagogue Gino Capponi (1792-1876), with another point of view, but pointing towards divine influence in education, wrote "that education is ultimately revelation, when he indicated that "God reveals himself in the heart of mothers for a mystery of affection; "Also the education of men is a mystery and is made up of affections..." (Taken from Nicola Abbagnano, A. Visalberghi. 1992, p. 365)

From the evolutionary point of view, the innatism of education is based on the fact that the species inferior to man in the evolutionary chain teach their offspring the basics so that they can defend themselves in the environment that surrounds them; no one puts in question that "animals teach their young to survive until they can fend for themselves" (Consuelo Martínez Priego, 2008, p. 74).

Animals give "instructions" to their young so that they feed and protect themselves from predators. This maintenance or protection behavior is expressions of instinctive affection. In their coexistence with other members of their species, they must learn to "respect" spaces of domination that the leaders of the packs have; this "teaches" them that their actions have certain limits, unless they want to impose themselves by force.

When the animal evolves into a man, it carries with it in its genetic and mental structure the need to teach its children. As man evolved and lived in community, he incorporated norms of coexistence that became guiding principles or values to live in harmony with his fellow human beings. But he also incorporated those behaviors of protection and maintenance of the offspring, expressed in "maternal love" (which is also paternal), an affection that is characteristic even in prehistoric tribes. The functions of this education were to instruct, train and socialize the values to face the hard life of their historical moment. And the objective or reason for being was individual and collective adaptation to its environment, and the survival of the species. This education, carried out from instinctive maternal love, involves training a person, and to be such, a person must be free and independent in harmony with his or her context and community.

NA Konstantinov., EN Mediski, MF Shabaeva (s/f, p. 4), even when they question the biological or evolutionary position of education, because they consider that education arose from labor activity of primitive man and the social relations that were established around it, expressed:

Handling in a very detailed manner data obtained exclusively in the animal world, and due to the "concern" of adults in transmitting to new generations the habits of adaptation to the environment, the supporters of these conceptions (for example, SH Laturneau and A. Thorns) identify the instinctive actions of animals with the educational practices of primitive man and arrive at the incredible conclusion that at the base of education lies an instinctive tendency of man to perpetuate the species, which acts as a law of selection natural.

A modern example of what was expressed by NA Konstantinov., IN Medinsky, MF Shabaeva, It has been implemented by Bunker Roy in 1972, in the Village of Tilonia, Rajasthan, in India; it is called Barefoot College, whose purpose is for illiterate people or people without university degrees to teach the members of the rural community to solve their daily problems,with the aim of making them self-sufficient. They do not give titles, certificates, etc.; the work activities learned modify their personality, contribute to their freedom. The motivation for this education is the genuine interest in helping others, it is based on social affection for others. However, this does not contradict the innate character of education, it only reinforces the thesis that intentional, systematic education, when given with the appropriate motivation (according to circumstances, context) is positive in achieving natural and artificial purposes.

The thesis of innatism of Education is corroborated by Juan Amós Comenio (1998) when he points out: "It is a principle accepted by all that man is born with the aptitude to acquire knowledge of things, in the first place because he is the image of God. The image, if it is faithful, must represent and reproduce all the features of its model, otherwise it would not be a true image" (p. 9). "Aristotle affirmed that the desire to know was innate in man" (p. 32).

Currently, the jungle communities or tribes of the American Amazon or Africa, which have had little or no interaction with the influences of modernity, and also any modern home in the rest of the world, are other empirical evidence of the innatism of education; They support the instinctive act of the human being to educate, that is, to instruct and moralize his descendants (some add the act of training and socializing) from the affections between them. The natural environment where this process takes place is the home, and it extends to the tribe or community. This is why the saying that "education begins at home" was born. Natural education is generally an education of individuals, natural education is an education motivated by the affections between teachers and learners.

Now, the innate characteristics of natural education developed for society also occur in the history of an individual. Natural education is carried out intensively in the first years of his life, with the consequent limitations. Currently, the State and other private agencies are intervening powerfully in this part of the process, due to the influence of modern psychology, which has considered this period as the most important in the development of the person. Artificial education, developed in the first years of the individual's life that follows the essential guidelines of natural education, is very successful. When artificial education lacks the fundamental motivation of natural education, it causes harm to the child. Natural education is an education from life to life. It is an education based largely on affection.

It is in this line of analysis that the Organization for Economic Cooperation and Development (OECD)(2003, p. 26)states, "effective learning, which begins at birth and continues into old age, grants each individual the best hope for a successful life," shows not only where education begins, but also the need to seriously address this vision. This opinion of the OECD is similar to that of the great American pedagogue John Dewey (1977), when he points out that education is a process "that begins unconsciously, almost at the moment of birth, and that incessantly shapes the faculties of the individual, saturating their conscience, forming their habits, exercising their ideas and awakening their feelings and emotions" (p. 55). The two opinions indicate one aspect of the innatism of education: the innatism of education only at the level of the history of the individual; without making reference to education as a social historical fact.

It is interesting to note that, since natural education is an innate activity and whose essential motivation is the love between the one who teaches and the one who learns, a role is automatically assigned to the educator: that of being a father (mother) or that of a friend. This relationship makes it easier to express affection for the other, to be interested in their development and well-being.

In summary, the characteristics of natural education are:

- His nativism.
- The fundamental motivation of this education is the love or affection between teachers and learners.
- Have unrationalized intentionality.
- Develop a spontaneous, unplanned communication interaction.
- To constitute a social practice whose final result is to train a person for the corresponding purposes.

- The educator is fundamentally vocational, instinctive.

As social organization becomes more complex, when families and tribes become larger communities, education ceases to be a family or tribal concern, education becomes more widespread, escapes the scope of the home, and, without denying or eliminating the first stage, A second stage of education develops, an artificial education, organized and directed by the State (or other corporations, such as churches, companies, etc.), an education socialized in larger groups. Artificial education constitutes the educational foundation of a society. Contrary to natural education, artificial education is an institutionalized education, with intentionality-rationalized, organic, systematic, formal, and generally directed by institutionalized power groups (read State, churches, economic corporations).

Artificial education is not an education for an individual, but an education for the masses. This characteristic prompted the development of theoretical proposals to define how it should be educated. Based on these proposals, professional preparation of the educator was required to entrust the lives of millions of people to him. So the educator was professionalized; that is, they were now teachers. Other currents emphasized the educator's role as teachers, calling them teachers. Beyond their names, the truth is that a large percentage of these educators became teachers or "occasional" teachers and not vocational ones. For this reason, it is understood why occasional educators do not have the "natural" motives to contribute to the formation of people based on an affectionate relationship. Their motivations for exercising such a function are different; they have to do with social or economic recognition, or the fulfillment of administrative objectives.

This intellectualist characteristic of artificial education shapes the role of teachers in the educational process. Some examples illustrate this assertion: If an educational process based on educational tradition is followed, the role assigned to the teacher will be that of an expert, magistrocentrism will prevail. If the theoretical proposal highlights educational technology, the role of the teacher will be that of a behavioral engineer, one who is concerned with using technology to modify the behavior of students. If non-directive education predominates, the role assigned to the teacher is that of learning facilitator, etc. All this "intellectualism" produced a "forgetting" or undervaluation of the role of the educator in natural education: being a parent or friend, because it was also "forgotten" that the foundation of natural education is the affection that must be manifested between teachers and learners.

The differences between natural and artificial education relative to the components of the educational process are basically in the educational objectives. In natural education, depending on the perspective, the objectives were to be happy by being right with God or to train to survive in community. While in artificial education the educational objectives will vary depending on the complexity or ideology of the society being analyzed; In many cases the natural objectives of education will be modified "or forgotten"

The educational objectives proposed in artificial education generally obey the "genius", inspiration or goals of the identification systems of the intellectuals of the power groups (call them the State, intellectual community, political or economic groups, tribal chiefs, heads of family etc.), so that the objectives or functions attributed to education will be as numerous as the intellectuals who dare to incorporate something original or different from what is established.

Therefore, in each society a different type of educational objectives is imposed. For example, García A. Lorenzo (1989, p. 14-19) indicates in table No. 1 how each intellectual highlights the objectives that education must meet, which was surely implemented in his time and society:

Table nº 1 Objectives of education according to theorists:

Authors	Improvement	Intentional	Faculty Human	Influence	End	Aid	Self-realization	Socialization	Process activities	Driving	Communication
Aristotle					X					X	
Azevedo								X	X		X
Belth											X
Bittencourt							X	X	X		
white rufino	X	X	X		X		X	X		X	
cohn	X	X		X							
Comte								X			
copperman	X							X	X		
Couffignal											X
Dante					X						
Debesse						X	X				
Dewey								X			X
Dilthey	X	X		X					X		
Durkheim	X							X			
Flitner	X	X		X					X		
Fröbel	X					X	X		X		
Garcia sickle	X	X	X								
Glezalvarez	X		X								
Gottler	X			X		X	X	X			
Henz			X	X			X	X			
Herbart	X			X						X	
Hubert	X	X		X	X				X		
James w.								X			
Joy	X	X	X	X							
Kant	X		X								
Kerschensteiner							X				
Kilpatrick							X	X	X		
Lemus	X				X		X				
Locke			X		X						
Manjon	X		X								
Cashew					X						
james mill					X						

stuart mill	x										x
Nassif	x			x							
Natorp	x						x				
Overberg	x									x	
Pestalozzi	x	x	x						x		
iron		x		x	x				x		
Plato	x		x								
Ruiz loved	x	x						x			
Spencer	x				x				x		x
Spranger	x			x		x					
Suchodolski	x				x			x			
Tusquet	x		x		x						
Willmann	x	x		x				x			
Zaragueta				x			x		x		
Ziller		x					x		x		

Other differences between natural and artificial education, considering the components of the educational process, are given by the contents that are shared, in the organization of the process, in the presence or absence of components such as evaluation, reasoned methods or strategies, planning of the process. etc

1.2.2 Common characteristics between natural and artificial education.

The first common characteristic is that there are similar components of education in these two types of education.

A. The first similar component is that there are systemic areas; Natural education generally occurs in natural systems such as the family, in related circles such as friends, etc., and artificial education generally occurs in artificial systems such as school, business.

B. The second common characteristic is that they have the same basic functions: instruct and moralize.

C. Another common element in natural and artificial education is that the educational act is summarized in the process of teaching and learning (but valued learning – intentional); Those who feel or have the authority to teach (parents, social leaders, teachers, etc.) share their experiences or knowledge with those who are obliged to learn (children, students, etc.). A third common component is that in the educational act, not only content is exchanged, but also feelings; there is a positive or negative relationship of will between teachers and learners.

D. Another important common characteristic, from ideality, although reality often contradicts this educational ideal, is that education is taught (from what is natural or artificial) so that the person acquires a certain degree of independence, autonomy and freedom, with the purpose that Live well, may it develop according to your aspirations and efforts. That is the long-term objective. The reality, especially in artificial education, is that, in many places in the world, in many schools, education is taught to domesticate, to "robotize," a fact that occurs due to a misinterpretation of the teacher's role or due to the mediocrity of the teachings. people who will serve as teachers in educational institutions of all levels. Deforming the person not only goes against the nature of education, but is harmful to humanity.

E. **Education is a socio-cultural and political process, where power groups impose the objectives and contents..** From a very ideologized perception, Giovanni Bechelloni (1977) says,

An identical dissimulation imposes the culture of the dominant classes as legitimate. But the school makes its own the particular culture of the dominant classes, masks its social nature and presents it as the objective, indisputable culture, rejecting at the same time the cultures of other social groups. The school legitimizes cultural arbitrariness in such a way (p. 4.)

In this work we agree with the fact that culture is imposed and legitimized by dominant groups through school education, but we do not agree when it is pointed out that the only purpose is to reproduce, correspond or resist the social order in school (depending on whether one is a supporter of the theories of Reproduction of Bourdieu and Passeron, or the Resistance of Althusser Baudelot and Establet, or the theory of Correspondence of Herbert Gintis). School, especially basic training, is not the most appropriate space to reproduce the structures and relationships of society or to resist it. Ideology is not generally the reason that leads to reproducing certain social behaviors in school; the most influential reason is the mediocrity of the person who works as a teacher. A well-prepared teacher, aware of her social function, promotes the child's freedom: freedom to think, freedom to act. In many countries of the world, the teacher is more of an occasion than a vocation.

The imposition of components in education (values, content or, in general terms, culture) is a less ideologized concept. The perspective is more operational, more organizational, and occurs in the two stages of education (natural education and artificial education); it is a reflex act of the "discipline" that molds the child in the principles and values of society. To a certain extent, in the early stages of natural and artificial education, imposition is a necessity, so that it incorporates in children certain knowledge and values that give them a sense of identity and belonging with the family and the society in which they live. When imposition becomes a way of educating without respecting the growth of man as a person, when everything is "discipline", limitation; then, imposition becomes a disturbing instrument, a distorter in the formation of the human being's conscience.

The contents and values are imposed by the State through its educational system in all its forms and organizations (schools, institutes, universities), to turn people into correct and useful citizens; but it also imposes certain rules of conduct, such as order. If this is true, then the problem is in its instrumentalization. The operators (occasional teachers) if they are not imbued with the spirit of education, they prevent the student's free expression and limit their freedom of thought. And with this the objectives set are frustrated.

It is also imposed by the market, with its different pressure mechanisms, so that its values of competition and efficiency guide the lives of individuals. The market requires training human resources or effective instruments for its own purposes. Incredible as it may seem, the market has greater influence than the State in ensuring that official operators meet their objectives.

It is imposed by parents, with the best of their intentions and intuitions, in order for their children to develop as people of whom they are proud. It is imposed by the church in order to keep the membership in order. It is imposed by the media to develop certain generally consumerist behaviors, imposing the value of "having more." Finally, It is imposed by friends to establish norms of group coexistence.

Therefore, education, in any of its components and in any of the stages, is imposed with subtlety from micro spatial areas such as in the family, to macro spatial areas such as in a Continent; an example of the latter occurs with the agreements of the Bologna declaration:

> *The adaptation to the Bologna process has been linked in Spain, in the new design and structure of university degrees, to the discourse of "skills". Uncritically, the Tuning Educational structures in Europe project (González and Wagenaar, 2003) has been adopted, initially, as a base model for curricular design in the degree reform.*

Indicating that it is imposed by power groups is not assessing whether it is good or bad, but it does indicate the responsibility of these groups or the State, and also, the role of educational operators. The people consciously or unconsciously accept this imposition, but, when they act consciously, the processes are more efficient and the results are more forceful, since they participate knowing that they play a role, and they understand that their participation, whether as agents of change or supervision is necessary in the transformation of education.

It is necessary to add that there is only one moment in the educational process when the values or contents of education are not imposed, when these components are negotiated or rejected, and that is when the person imposes on himself what he selects. That is, when the subject takes on a level of consciousness that allows him or her to be free, therefore, to be different for the better. Unfortunately, the individual with that level of consciousness, and the educational processes that stimulate or form consciousness for people's self-development, are very rare. However, this type of education generates permanent fruits, because it was oneself who provisionally decided, who selected what was good for oneself.

This type of education gives feelings of freedom, emancipation, generates critical capacity and creativity, the human being develops, grows as a person. This is how Nivia Álvarez and Agustín de la Herrán (2009, p. 15) expressed it: "when you come to know, to understand that self-knowledge is the first step to growth as human beings, that there is no other way out, then you assumes consciously and responsibly." And this is how Alfred Whitehead defined it in his book "The Aims of Education" (1929), when he pointed out that the objective of education is to become aware of this process. In a way it should be considered "religious" because it develops a sense of duty and reverence.

So, an education based on collective interest and of a systematic-rigid nature versus an education based on the autonomy of the person and systematic flexibility, based on their experience and knowledge, apparently are antagonistic and exclusive types of education. Fortunately, this second proposal is not a utopia, which only remains for speculative or theoretical reflection. Paul Robert (s/a, p.3), Director of the Nelson Mandela School, in Clarensac Gard, France, pointed out that:

The idea that a happy, well-developed student, free to progress at his own pace, will more easily acquire fundamental knowledge is not a utopia of an enlightened pedagogue: it is simply the idea that guides the action of everyone: the State, the Municipalities, the School Directors, the teachers [...] Finland deeply respects knowledge, but it respects even more the individuals who are in the process of acquiring it. And that is not considered there as a dull idealism, but rather as the most basic pragmatism. Esa Räty, Director of the Niinivaara school in Joensuu, assumes as his motto the formula that summarizes this philosophy: 'every student is important'.

Education in Finland has that intention, that is, orienting education towards developing the consciousness of the individual.

A different explanatory vision, but similar in establishing the difference in educational trends, is the one proposed by Leticia Barrios Graziani (2007), when she says that,

Post-rationalist theories discuss the rigidities of the educational model and its inability to capture multiple aspects of intelligence, as well as the various aspects involved in the teaching-learning process. Initially we will find the configuration of an alternative paradigm to the rationalist model based on a humanist conception of education, which is inspired and supported by holistic and positive integrative visions of the human being. This paradigm will evolve towards anti-rational and individualistic positions that make it very questionable in the field of education. Which makes it necessary to demand different alternatives to this paradigm based on a balanced rationalism and a conception that is both humanistic and supportive. Finally, although the criticism and questioning of post-rationalist theories of the rationalist model are correct and fair, they have evolved towards reactionary thinking, becoming a kind of "subculture" that matches the current phase of capitalism and thought. neoliberal. In short, post-rationalism ends up promoting an individualistic and self-

marginalizing culture that effectively contributes to the stability of the system.

F. Another biological foundation in education is the participation of brain processes in education; the contributions of neuroscience are vital in this matter, applicable to natural and artificial education. Neurophysiology, for example, explains that the analytical, creative, logical, etc. activities of the human being are conditioned by the development of the cerebral hemispheres or specific areas of the brain, and also by the biochemical activity in the neurons.

Teaching and learning involve an interaction between the cultural and mental worlds using the human brain as a mediator. The brain is the physical support for developing mental processes, and the mind catalyzes the processes of elaboration, interpretation and representation of a perceived reality. Furthermore, in the brain (limbic system) the human being's emotions are conditioned, and moods condition the way one teaches, and the quantity-quality of what one learns. The neurophysiological structure of the brain (biological) clearly influences education, it allows us to communicate in all directions, it allows us to see, hear, feel, etc.

Education as a biological process is conditioned by the action of the areas of the brain, and without whose knowledge we would not understand learning pathologies such as: visual and auditory aphasia, dyslexia, dyscalculis, agnosia in all its varieties, etc., but it also highlights the importance of certain mental processes, such as memory, so reviled in recent times.

G. Another common property or characteristic of education is its historical and complex character. Not only of the external history of education, accepted and promoted, but of the internal history, that of the individual and society that is impregnated in the development of the person. A story that develops in particular circumstances or contexts. Saverio Fausto de Dominicis

(1846-1930), highlighted the historical character of education, from the collective point of view, emphasizing its conditioning with the political-social situation, indicating that, "just as it would be absurd to want to educate and instruct a people with ideas not appropriate to its historical development, it is absurd to want to base the instruction of an era, different from previous ones, on intellectual and moral fragments from other eras" (p. 390).

Fernando Savater (1997) points out this historical connotation, referring to what education transmits from the point of view of the individual:

The second thing is that we are not the initiators of our lineage, that we appear in a world where the human footprint is already in force in a thousand ways [...]; but he will also learn that these similar people are all in fact present to us, that many have already died and that nevertheless their discoveries or their struggles continue to count for him as vital lessons. [...]. The temporal panorama is the counterweight to our awareness of inexorable death [...]. Through education we are not born into the world but into time: we are loaded with symbols and past fames[...] the function of teaching is so essentially rooted in the human condition that it is forced to admit that anyone can teach(pp. 38-40).

Just as a person's life is a continuum, that person's education is also a continuum. In the individual, natural education and artificial education are part of a single process, education is for life. Man is a social and biological being, constituted by his neurophysiological experience and his social experience, which is materialized in the personality of the subject. A being that can be formed, deformed and reformed at any stage of his life, if he wishes. As you can see, the key is him; Therefore, it is important that the individual becomes aware of the importance of his/her SELF. This social and neurophysiological experience forms a personality, which makes him different, and which should generate a free man to live well with himself, with the community and with his environment.

> H. Natural and artificial education is complex: Complex due to the number of components, complex due to the organizational breadth, due to the configuration of its processes and from the participation of different scientific and technical disciplines. This complexity generates a wealth of analysis, a breadth of topics to investigate, and a contribution from many disciplines to better understand and explain the educational process. Complexity allows education to be studied systemically, both holistically and each component or subprocess. This property of education itself enriches your research and reflection.

Education, in any of its stages, has two dimensions: As a social process and as an individual fact. However, education as a social process has two sub-dimensions:

1. The vertical sub-dimension, where society through its social actors and institutions imposes training or deformation on people through systematic education, also known as official or formal education, or unsystematic or informal education.
2. The horizontal sub-dimension, where the person interacts with others and exchanges content, experiences, values, attitudes. In this dimension, a person contributes to others in their training processes.

Now, education as an individual fact is imposed or self-imposed. When the individual imposes self-imposed objectives, content, etc., it is because he has become aware of his role in life and in society. This type of education is the ideal education that occurs at the highest level of maturity of the individual. We could interpret, with the logic of A. de la Herrán (1998), that the student is aware of his own learning, aware of the commitments acquired and therefore capable of undertaking and modifying the unfair and disturbing reality.

The misunderstanding or lack of understanding of educational objectives and education as a continuous social process and individual fact, creates a series of problems. First, that the educational process has gaps or breaks, often contradictory. Second, there is no necessary complementation in the continuum of his life, and thus respond favorably to the demands of today's world, causing trauma or difficulties to successfully incorporate into his daily life. Third, that their natural objectives or those generated artificially are not adequately executed by educational operators (parents, teachers, etc.), distorting or betraying them, for example, when political or economic interests prevail that seek to "domesticate", "robotize" or homogenize groups of people. It is therefore a necessity and an obligation to reflect and know the educational process to achieve its transformation for the benefit of people and society.

1.3 Education as an object of study

The last common characteristic between natural and artificial education is that they constitute an object of study, studied by various disciplines and from many points of view. Education as an object of study is studied to be explained, but it is also studied to be transformed, the first enters the field of science and the second in the field of technology. Reynaldo Suarez Díaz (1995, p.12) gives us an idea of how to study education, indicating

The following dimensions: the philosophy of education that studies the purpose of education; the sociology of education the educational act that describes the context, educational psychology that deals with the subject of education; the educational methodology that would deal with the materials and methods, and the contribution of other sciences as content or knowledge to share in the teaching-learning process.

Paciano Fermoso (1985, p. 22) gives us another perspective on how to study education, pointing out that

The technical knowledge about education is 'Didactics', 'School Organization' and 'Educational Technology'; Scientific knowledge is 'Pedagogy' or 'Science of Education'; philosophical knowledge is the 'Philosophy of Education'; and theological knowledge, the 'Theology of Education'. All these disciplines study education, but under different aspects, at a different cognitive level and under a different formality.

To graph the nature of education and the way of studying it, adapting Paciano Fermoso's proposal, I suggest likening education to a river. Education and the river have an origin (education has an origin as a social process applied to humanity, as applied to the individual). Then, at the beginning it is just a stream and in the course it becomes the river itself, education at the beginning of humanity or the individual is informal, non-systematic, and then it continues to be systematic and formal. The river is basically made up of water particles, in the same way education is made up of educational facts, and it is these when they are ordered to generate an educational function that constitutes the educational processes.

Just as the river has streamlines or flow lines that go at different speeds, in education, the flow lines are the educational processes that range from training, teaching, organization, etc. The river and education have flow lines with different importance (in education there are different subprocesses with different hierarchy and importance, for example, the process of training people is more important than the political and organizational processes in education). In the stream, planes of the same identity are not perceived; in natural education these levels or differentiations are not perceived; however, the constituted river does have different planes or levels, superficial, intermediate, deep currents, the same thing, the formal educational system. They also have different levels or levels (basic education, higher education, etc.). The river and education can be studied or worked on from different perspectives that generate different knowledge. For example, in the river: the knowledge that can be obtained is given from the hydraulic perspective, fluid mechanics, hydrology, or professional procedures to channel the river, etc.; in education, it can be studied from the philosophical, scientific, technical and artistic plane (see graph No. 1).

Graph No. 1 Different knowledge that is generated when considering Education as an object of study.

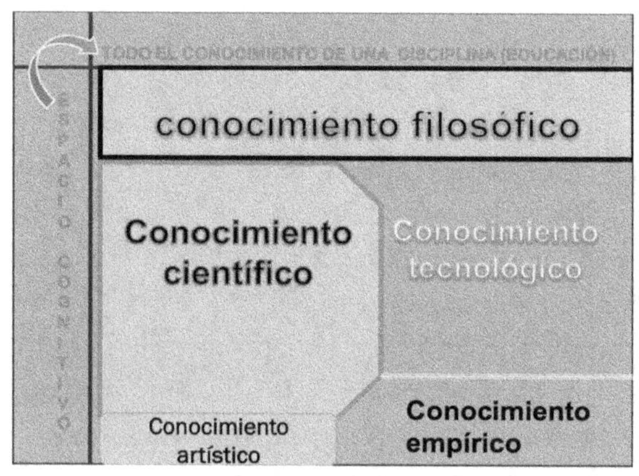

Just as describing the river from an airplane will provide very general information, more about the form than its details, so philosophizing about education will generate very generic reflections on it; The discipline that provides this type of information is Philosophy of Education. On another level, walking along the river, analyzing and examining it provides more detailed information about the nature of the river, in the same way, through scientific research, a more detailed description and a more complete explanation of education will be obtained; The discipline that provides this information is Educational Science or Pedagogy. With the previous study, the river is intervened, it is transformed; The river is looked at from a more utilitarian point of view, but a set of normative propositions for its transformation are also developed; This type of knowledge and action that transforms the reality of education is called Educational Technology or Didactics. At the same time you can paint the river or create poems or books; this information is artistic, different from philosophical, scientific and technological knowledge.

If we accept that education is innate and studyable, why don't we enhance the competitive advantage that this means, having in-depth knowledge about it? First: to instruct from affection and moralization; We must select the cultural content and values in accordance with our aspirations that we as a society agree on, content that must be useful and practical. Second: Share cultural content with the aim of developing the learner's consciousness, to achieve self-learning; It is progressively giving it freedom, similar to the freedom that must be given to a spring that is compressed to know its exact location, since if it is abruptly released it will go anywhere. Third, Coordinate the different stages of education (innate and artificial or systematic), and also the different phases of systematic education with the objective set by society. And finally, give your best thinking about helping the learner, maintaining the joy of learning, strictly speaking, allowing them to be happy.

Another yes, the history of civilizations shows that peoples who had tranquility, calm and development managed to harmonize instruction and moralization in a strategic balance. And when an imbalance was generated then the results were calamitous, such as the Babylonian, Greek, Roman, etc. empires. When analyzing the state of today's society, where we live with increasingly common acts of violence, with crime that borders on the most extreme perversion of man, with increasingly complex human pathologies (pedophilia, suicide to compete, etc.), the increased level of individual and corporate corruption that undermines the foundations of society, etc., one wonders why society is at such a low level of humanization with the paradox of living in the highest degree of knowledge through the development of science and technology? Let's try some answers:

1. Knowledge, read science, only deals with the external or internal phenomena of the subject to describe, explain or understand them, and technology is concerned with transforming the subject's environment, with making life easier, but neither of the two .It is concerned with transforming the subject itself.

2. Knowledge, read science and technology, and if we were to use the human body metaphorically as a simile of humanity, only develops the brain and limbs, but almost nothing the heart. That is to say, we have a robust and intelligent human body, very useful for certain things but useless for a good coexistence, because it is almost devoid of values, positive feelings.

3. Natural action (natural and instinctive education) and the most transcendent human invention (artificial education) are important instruments to strategically combine the development of the "brain and limbs with the heart", but, in part due to the "madness of man" the development of some "organs" began to be privileged at the expense of others; so that we had a great brain and atrophied limbs and a weak heart, or a great brain and powerful limbs but a failing heart. The obvious thing is that this body will malfunction, as happens with our society.

4. There are strange agents, "relatives of the human body with influence", such as the greedy market, unhealthy politics, that pressure to guarantee their survival, development and dominance, so that they "praise", support economically and with theories aimed at those governments that follow their "recommendations". We understand that the market,

the system, pressures to direct education in that direction, which is subtly reflected with Nietzsche masks, under propositions such as "educational quality is greater to the extent that we are more competent," or "society needs competent people." "; or "we must provide financial education to children" etc., "knowing more" has been privileged; which translates into the obsession of Latin American basic education to achieve better averages in the PISA tests. This situation forces us to answer ourselves before designing an educational system: should basic education be provided to satisfy the needs of society or the market? The market is only one of the social dimensions, it should not be the "almost everything" of a society.

5. Conclusion, a dysfunctional body similar to a dysfunctional society like ours cannot continue in this trend without the risk of gradually self-destructing. The instructive component of education is not enough to constitute a civilized, humane society with good coexistence. This would not be any problem if the same importance or equal attention were given to the moralizing, affective part in education; but no, instruction prevails over everything. This explains, because it is embedded in the collective consciousness: "No problem, steal but do something" or "as long as it makes us profit, it doesn't matter how you do it" etc. If we want to avoid the cliff that the current situation guides us, it is necessary to take the steps again, what we have to do is EDUCATE, from natural education and artificial education, guided by the wise strategic balance of instructing and moralizing. What does this imply?

1.4 Definition of Education

As a final reflection, a definition of education is postulated, which considers the regularities of this social process, regularities that are observed in all societies; regardless of whether they have gone through different phases or stages, from primitive society, feudal society, to the information society or digital society. The definition that is postulated contains its essential characteristics and the natural objectives intact, and admits the variation of the artificial objectives depending on the cultural differences that particular societies have, seeking to emphasize the strategic balance in education between instruction and moralization.

The proposed synthetic conception of education is:

Education is a social, biological and cultural process, whose natural or primary objective is to instruct and moralize human beings, that is, to contribute to the formation of people, and its artificial or secondary objectives will depend on the society where it is educated, since It depends on the interest of the power groups and the educational level in question.

Education as an action external to the subject only contributes to forming him, and it is because we must accept that in normal situations, the SUBJECT is the protagonist of his own formation.

To conclude these reflections, some clarifications to the terminology used that has not been analyzed previously. In the educational academic world there is a serious discussion about the central objective of education: education forms men or education forms people. Although they seem similar, there are subtle differences. The position in this work is that education forms people before forming man, not only because the person involves a formation of rationality-morality and emotionality, but also for the reasons detailed below:

- From the semantic level, when referring to the person, it implies giving due importance to the development of judgment, thought, will, conscience, and reason of the human being. To form a person is to highlight the formation of individuals from and with the affections that are exchanged between teachers and learners. Referring to man implies highlighting his nature, his natural condition, the physical, the birth of being, the material.

- From the sociological level, man is born a subject, an individual. This is not the ideal state of the human, the human is a gregarious being, he needs to live with others, he requires socializing with his fellow humans, that is, the subject must become a person, he becomes a person through his interrelation with others. Training people involves training man in his relationship with humanity in a specific context, without destroying his individuality.

- From the ontological level, man in his human nature manifests himself as a person or as an individual. If individuality predominates, man disperses and becomes a thing, he becomes dehumanized, since the individual lives by and for himself. However, man is fully realized if his personality predominates, that is, his characterization as a human being in relation to his environment and others. In fact, the I without the we is far from being true, just as the we without the I has no meaning. Being the person an end in himself, he generates an ontologically worthy reality.

- From the anthropological level, man, as an incarnated reality, exists in the world and history as part of a mass; the conformist, faceless, manipulated amorphous mass absorbs the man-thing, the man-object, the utilitarian man. The realization of man as a person takes place in the community, there HE is important, there he transcends his own existence, discovering the meaning of his life, this gives him uniqueness and originality in the world.

- The neurological level illustrates this subtle difference, for example Alzheimer's disease, a disease that damages brain cells and therefore the processes of thought and rationality. The result of this painful disease shows us that as men they continue with their existence, but as people they are losing their validity, since their substantive and essential characteristics such as learning, the use of their will, conscience and reason become inactive.

By establishing that Education, in its natural and artificial character, requires training people, it helps to challenge the approach of some theorists of highlighting the "contributor of training" (read teacher or teaching) or of putting all the emphasis on the "trained person." (read student or learning). This pendulum theoretical behavior generates a false and unnecessary conflict between teaching and learning, which has led to the distortion of educational processes, especially in Artificial Education. What matters is establishing the balance between teaching and learning, according to the needs of the students and the levels in the educational process.

The concrete thing is that the central axis of any educational process is to train the person, and teaching, learning and their interaction must lead to training, and not deformation. So, if on some occasions, to train the educator must transmit information then it must be done, and if learning must be facilitated so that they build their personality (individual or professional), then do it, or if the experiences must only be experienced then we do not let's oppose This is the participation of the "trainer" in the educational process, knowing what role he or she must play at each moment of the educational process. On the other pole, if the "trained" person has to learn by constructing new concepts or behaviors then they are welcome, just as if they had to unlearn deep-rooted concepts or behaviors. Unlearning implies not only a rational act, which is what is commonly known as learning, but also a fight against one's values, prejudices, and emotions. Teaching-learning has the sole purpose of forming a good person, according to the canons of the family, group, or society in particular.

What is necessary to highlight is that, in reality, the natural objectives, instructing and moralizing, are sufficient to form a person in a simple society. Artificial and natural education must not forget that it must be taught from affection, be it the student, the child, the friend, or the parishioner. If the teacher does not have the conditions to behave as a second "father or mother" to his students, the least he should do is behave as a "friend" to his students. That is, cultivating affection of any type and intensity for those with whom we interact with the sole objective of contributing to the formation of a good person. That is the role that natural education assigns to the educator: being a parent or friend. While artificial education assigns the educator the role of expert, facilitator, mediator, or leader. Artificial education is enhanced when the teacher or professor fulfills the role of friend at the relevant moments.

To live well for oneself and in society, one only needs to have information and values to guide our decisions. However, in a complex society, where games of interests operate (individual, group, business, political, etc.), and where psychological-somatic pathologies, typical of modernity, have also been incorporated, such as anxiety, stress, natural objectives are insufficient. Everyday experience constantly shows that rationality and morality are insufficient to explain a person's behavior. Today, the emotional formation of the human being must be complemented in the process of moralization, much more in artificial education than in natural education (because here parents who raise well do something), especially when they must unlearn or confront selfish interests.

THE NATURE OF PEDAGOGY

Pedagogy has become a topic of great controversy. What is it? Science, Technology, Art or everything together? Is it the science of education or is it part of Educational Sciences? How to conceptualize Pedagogy? What conceptual tools could be used to establish its real nature?

CHAPTER 2

THE NATURE OF PEDAGOGY

One of the main objectives of education should be to expand the windows through which we see the world.

— ARNOLD GLASOW

Currently, the term pedagogy is used interchangeably for many things and objectives, from relating pedagogy to the control of each action in the educational process, to understanding it as teaching strategies, to providing it with a philosophical approach. Its current polysemy due to the lack of agreements, which should occur in an international debate, generates such imprecision that it requires a study of its nature.

No one disputes the etymological meaning of the term "Pedagogy" (from the Greek paidós = child and agogy = conduction), nor its historical content: relating to the pedagogue, a Greek slave who in Hellenized Rome led or guided his master's children to a training institution (gymnasium,didaskáleia), to the theater etc., not only to protect them but also to guide their behavior, so that they behave with good manners. Slaves had little to do with intellectual training. Currently, referring to Pedagogy from its etymology would be a very serious error, the etymological meaning does not describe or cover the fields of action.

From Sophocles (495-406 BC) until today, it is clear that the concept of Pedagogy has evolved and has been modified on two levels:

a. From its object of interest: first, it was exclusively children, today it has incorporated other actors: adolescents, young people, and adults.

b. From its actions: Originally, it referred to physical action, currently Pedagogy refers more to a branch of knowledge related to the formation of the person.

Regarding the second dimension, its reconceptualization has been clearer. After describing the original physical action, Pedagogy was then considered as an educational practice (giving it the character of an art of education). He continued his metamorphosis by including details of procedures to improve the art of teaching and learning (giving it an educational technology character). Faced with the empire of philosophy, many intellectuals related Pedagogy with the Theory of Education, dedicating themselves to reflecting on the telos and onto of education, giving it the character of Philosophy of education. When historically the center of social attention changed, leaving the primacy of philosophy and putting science first, many intellectuals strove to characterize Pedagogy as a science, seeking to explain every educational fact.

Regarding this last point, there are basically two aspects: one that calls Pedagogy the Science of Education, and the other, which considers Pedagogy as part of the Sciences of Education. The evolution of the concept of Pedagogy, which can be perceived throughout its history, is closely related to the cultural development of humanity.

2.1 CONCEPTS OF PEDAGOGY

The conceptual evolution of Pedagogy has not been linear or simple, and this is due to the complexity of society, the differentiated cultural and ideological advance in different societies, the development of productive and cultural structures, which have undoubtedly influenced the intellectuals of each era to develop the concept. On this basis, many specialists on the subject, in a certain historical space-time, referred to Pedagogy as an artistic, technological, scientific or philosophical discipline, and many others, as a combination of them, in the belief that evolution cultural did not lose the characteristics acquired over time. Currently, these conceptual differences persist regarding the nature of Pedagogy.

This lack of consensus and the multiplicity of its meanings make its understanding, and also the formation of a solid scientific community, very difficult; so that the appreciations of Pedagogy at the beginning of the 20th century, according to Hugo Münsterberg (1911, p. 2) was "the usual and truly unforgivable sin of pedagogical literature, is its vagueness," and having spent more than a century, in the conclusions of the book Fundamental Questions of Teaching, A. de la Herrán, J. Paredes, C. Moral Santaella, C. and T. Muñoz (2012), point out:

> *The scientific-social level has to do, as we say, with the little presence that Pedagogy has in our society, which should be, along with Medicine and Psychology, one of the closest and most popular sciences. Today Pedagogy is confused with Politics (dual or partisan), Pediatrics, Philosophy, Podiatry or Psychology [...] This state of generalized pedagogical ignorance characterizes (in its double sense of 'distinguishes' and 'disguises') this country where we live in a particular way [referring to Spain, my bold], saturating above all the levels of Secondary and University education, and from them to the majority of people and social systems, including families and the media (p. 714).*

This vagueness according to Münsterberg is generated in the scientific community of educators, and is due, among many reasons, to the imprecision, indefinition or multiplicity of meanings given to the concept "Pedagogy"; and pedagogical ignorance according to the contemporary authors reviewed occurs in Spanish society in general, in contrast to other social contexts in which Pedagogy is well known and appreciated, such as in Finland, Germany, Cuba, etc., where the educational level It is objectively remarkable. This explains, in some other contexts, the circulation of expressions that totally distort the nature of Pedagogy, such as, for example, "this action is pedagogical or this other is anti-pedagogical", since this exclusively relates Pedagogy to educational practice. , leaving aside the disciplinary, cognitive nature.

To certify the multiplicity of concepts, Lorenzo García Aretio (1989, pp. 35,36), professor of Pedagogy, is cited, who in a selected inventory of concepts to answer What is Pedagogy?, indicated, in alphabetical order:

BLANCO RUFINO (1930): "Science and art of education." "Certain and systematic knowledge of the essence, properties and relationships of education."

CASTILLEJO (1987): "Pedagogy is conceived as the science (theory) and technology of education."

COMPAYRE (1916): "Actually, no one doubts the possibility of a Science of Education anymore. Education is an art and involves more than abstract principles, but it needs them just as medicine needs medical sciences."

DERISI (1950): "Practical science located between pure speculative science, Philosophy of education and the mere art of the educator."

FAURE (1977): "Ancient art, new science. "Cultural process that seeks the emergence and development of all the virtualities of being."

GARCIA HOZ (1981): "Systematic set of demonstrated truths about education."

GOTTLER (1955): "Science of education...It must encompass all educational knowledge and must acquire it from determined sources with critical rigor and present it in the most perfect way possible, basing it on objective bases and inferring it whenever possible, in logical order." of supreme principles."

HUBERT (1984): Pedagogy aims to develop a doctrine of education, both theoretical and practical such as that of morality, of which it is an extension, and which is not exclusively science, nor technique, nor philosophy, nor art, but all of that together and ordered according to logical articulations."

KRIEK (1952): "It is a technology, it is a scientific theory of the technique of education and instruction."

MARIN IBAÑEZ (1984): "Pedagogy is the science and technique of education. Strictly speaking, pedagogy is scientific-reflective knowledge and its technological dimension is the projection and extension of its scientific character."

NASSIF (1980): "Pedagogy is the theory and technique of education."

PAULSEN (1927): "According to the form, two species of sciences can be distinguished: speculative and practical or technical. Pedagogy evidently belongs to the second group. It is the doctrine of an art; "the art of human formation".

PLANCHARD (1975): "Pedagogy is the science and art of education. It is descriptive science, normative theory, practical realization."

QUINTANA (1981): "Pedagogy is a science of education along with the other sciences of education, although distinguished from them by its scientific nature, and consequently, forming a separate group."

SAENZ (1986): "Pedagogy is a rational and disciplineable domain, that is, with scientific pretensions."

SAN JUAN (1983): "Pedagogy is the science of education."

SANVISENS (1984): "Pedagogy is science, technology, praxiology... Pedagogy has a scientific-philosophical dimension (founding), a technological dimension (mediating) and a praxiological dimension (applicative)."

SARRAMONA (1985) of technological sciences.

TITONE (1976): "Pedagogy is the study of the nature and

articulation of the educational process, that is, the systemic complex of concepts and principles that constitute the theory of education. It is practical-projective science."

VON CUBE (1981): "The definition of Pedagogy as a science of education seems more justified in the current use of language to me."

From another way of approaching the definition of Pedagogy, A. Rodríguez Martínez (2006) points out the conception of Pedagogy according to an interpretive framework that he called mentality or current, based on the proposal of JM Touriñan (1989, pp. 89-91). :

In this case, we are going to identify the Theory of Education in the Marginal mentality, also called experiential, philosophical-deductive or hermeneutic-dialectical [...] This leads us to identify, in this current, the Theory of Education with Philosophical Theories of Education and, consequently, the Theory of Education would be understood as the discipline of Philosophical Theories of Education. Examples of this way of understanding General Pedagogy are the works of D. Morando Pedagogía, or that of prof. O. Fullat Philosophers of Education. (p. 37, 39)

The Theory of Education in the subaltern mentality, also called interdisciplinary, of scientific studies of education or technical analysis [...] It is the field of study of Educational Sciences that can be defined as the "set of disciplines that study the conditions of existence, functioning and evolution of educational situations and facts" (Mialaret, 1977, p. 32), [...] Educational terms do not mean anything substantially different from what they mean in the generating disciplines that use them (since each one explains the part of the educational phenomenon that concerns it), that is, they have no intrinsic significance to the educational field. It is precisely in this sense that the supporters of this mentality maintain that an autonomous science of education is not possible, since the knowledge of education is not knowledge like that of other scientific disci-

plines, because the knowledge of Education is a type of knowledge that is obtained from the use of knowledge from consolidated disciplines, such as Biology, Psychology, Sociology, etc. [...] From this it can be deduced that in this current Pedagogy is more a technological knowledge that validates its subaltern technology through the theories of the generating disciplines (p.40, 41).

[...] According to this current, Educational Theory, as part of the knowledge of education, can be identified in three different ways.

- ***The Theory of Education as Philosophy of Education.*** *The Philosophy of Education should not be confused with the discipline of Philosophical Theories of Education of the marginal current [...] Therefore, the Theory of Education would be a special treatise on philosophy. The task is not specialized; what is specialized is the discipline.*
- ***Educational Theory as an Interpretive Theory.*** *They are special treatises on the different generating disciplines (Sociology, Psychology, Economics, Anthropology, Biology, History, etc.). All these generating disciplines have a theoretical-conceptual structure consolidated under scientific-technological rationality and explain educational activity based on the terms and concepts they develop to understand their own field of reality. Therefore, there will be as many interpretive theories as there are generating disciplines that study the field of reality education.*
- ***Educational Theory as Practical Theory.*** *We understand practical theories as rational constructions that direct action, combining socially or morally sanctioned goals or expectations, such as educational goals here and now for the student, with the means validated by interpretive theories. [...] When*

> *identifying the knowledge of education with Practical Theories, the Theory of Education is understood as a practical theory, also called Systematic Pedagogy, examples of this way of understanding General Pedagogy are the works of R. Hubert Treatise on Pedagogy General, by J. Gottler Systematic Pedagogy, R. Nassif General Pedagogy, etc. (Gottler, 1965; García Hoz, 1973; Hubert, 1970; Nassif, 1975; Henz, 1976). (p.44)*

Pedagogy is understood in this mentality or autonomous current or science of education as an autonomous scientific discipline because it is built based on its own object of study (education) using the scientific-technological form of knowledge, like the other disciplines. more consolidated autonomous scientific fields such as Physics, Biology, Psychology, Sociology, etc. That is, Pedagogy as a scientific discipline uses scientific-technological rationality in the field of education, understood as a reality with intrinsic significance in its terms). Developing, therefore, substantive theories of education and specific educational technologies (p. 45).

[...] After the above and taking into account what happens with other autonomous scientific disciplines, Pedagogy, like them, can be subdivided into different substantive academic disciplines. [...] Among the substantive academic disciplines of Pedagogy we can highlight: Social Pedagogy, School Organization, Didactics, Guidance and Diagnosis, Educational Theory (General Pedagogy), etc. [...]. In short, we understand that the only way to understand the Theory of Education or General Pedagogy is as a Substantive Academic Discipline of Pedagogy, that is, as part of Pedagogy as a science specific to the field of reality Education (p. 48).

The conclusion reached with the reading of A. Rodríguez Martínez (2006) based on JM Touriñan's proposal, whether we use the subaltern or autonomous mentality, is that Pedagogy should be a theoretical-practical science. What does that mean? That Pedagogy, being a theoretical-practical science, is an applied science? Or that Pedagogy, being a theoretical-practical science, is a technology? This name generates an epistemological problem, since science by its very nature is exclusively theoretical (whether it is called basic or applied science). And the only discipline of a practical nature that admits some theoretical components is Technology. So, is Pedagogy applied science or technology? Or is applied science the same as technology? Of course, this epistemological impasse will have to be resolved later.

Beyond the difficulty indicated in the previous paragraph, all the definitions of Pedagogy cited could be sufficient to know the state of the art on this topic. However, it never hurts to know the vision of other influential figures in the intellectual world, such as Hegel, Bachelard and other contemporary authors who offer us a broader range of the meaning of Pedagogy. And as in all things, the greater the abundance and difference of opinions, they could serve to confuse us (the glass half empty) or to enrich our analysis (the glass half full).

Nicola Abbagnano, A. Visalberghi (1992) points out that for Hegel, Pedagogy is Philosophy:

For Hegel, Pedagogy aims at the process by which the individual spirit rises to self-consciousness. This process is described as follows in the Phenomenology of the Spirit: "The individual must go through the degrees of formation of the universal spirit according to the figures set by the spirit, like degrees of a path already drawn and paved. In such a way, it happens that by observing what in previous ages kept the spirit of adults alert while now it is reduced to notions, exercises or even children's games, we recognize in the pedagogical process, almost as in projection, the history of civilization. ." From this point of view, education is the conquest, by the individual, of what the universal spirit has already conquered and accomplished.. (p.316)

F. T. Rink (1803) chooses a position regarding the nature of Pedagogy, indicating that it is an art.

Heart of education, originates mechanically in the variable occasions where we learn if something is useful or harmful to man. Every art of education that proceeds only mechanically must contain faults and errors, because it lacks a plan on which to base itself. The art of education or Pedagogy, needs to be reasoned 'if it is to develop human nature so that it can achieve its destiny (p. 3)

[...] Pedagogy or theory of education is either physical or practical. Physical education is what man has in common with animals, that is, care. Practical or moral education is that through which man must be formed to be able to live, as a being that acts freely. (p.7)

Dante Morando (1969), like Hegel, considers that Pedagogy is philosophical knowledge; it is the problem of its end: "it is a finalistic activity. It is a spiritual process, and the spirit does not appear by mistake" (p. 9). He further points out that education is an art, "it is not possible to determine what should be taught without a science of man and his educational purpose; while, however, it is possible to teach in fact, and also optimally, without knowing either systematically or scientifically how to teach" (p. 14).

Luis Piscoya Hermoza (1974, p.139, 140) states that Pedagogy is technology:

From the formal perspective, Pedagogy is prescriptive in nature and is made up of rules.[...]. Consequently, this structure of pedagogical rules turns out to be only a particular case of that of technological rules [...] it is inferred, without any difficulty, that Pedagogy is a technical discipline and that, therefore, its rules differ, essentially, of the statements belonging to scientific theories, because it does not make sense to attribute to them, as predicates, alethic values, that is, true – false.

Ferrandez – J. Sarramona (1980, p.3) describe the range of theoretical positions on Pedagogy:

The complexity of the educational process means that there are different positions on the concept of "science" or "sciences" of education.

For a group of authors, only Pedagogy is the only one that bears the name of Science of Education. All other subjects of study are simple ramifications of it; hence it cannot be called "pedagogical sciences." Along this line are Manzganiello, Planchard and Vexliard, among others.

Other authors admit that there are "other educational sciences" in addition to Pedagogy, which would be the general science of education. But these sciences would not have an independent character, but are subordinate to the first. [...] Authors such as García Hoz and Nassif can be cited here.

A third group is made up of those who admit the existence of a set of sciences related to education, but independent of each other as scientific disciplines. The common denominator of the educational sciences would be to have education as their formal objective, but addressing each of them from a different specific point of view, which gives them an entity of independence. Authors in favor of this opinion are: Clausse and García Garrido.

Finally, there are the authors who give the title of Educational Sciences to any science directly or indirectly related to the educational fact, although they do not have it as a specific object of study. Authors defending this opinion are: Debesse-Mialaret and Inif-Dovero.

OL Zuluaga (1987, p. 192) points out pedagogy as the "discipline that conceptualizes, applies and experiences knowledge related to the teaching of specific knowledge in different cultures. It emphasizes, on the one hand, the disciplinary, historical and social character of Pedagogy and, on the other, in the outstanding place of teaching as an "object" of articulation around which pedagogical reflection must focus its attention.

JI Bedoya Madrid. (2005, p.95) noted that:

For the epistemologist G. Bachelard, Pedagogy could never access the level of science because it always fulfills a function or is limited to being an activity (which is considered completely opposite to what would essentially define science). For Bachelard, Pedagogy understood only as the pedagogical process is something else different from science; it is again a practice of transmitting specific content with which it is intended to achieve only information or communication and through which, ultimately, it is about achieving a technical training and a domestication or ideological inculcation of the learning subject.

Josefa Zeballos (2010) points out that "Pedagogy is not exclusively science, technique, philosophy or art, but all of them at the same time. It is a practice based on scientific knowledge and technical skill that give purpose to the educational action." (p. 4). "Pedagogy is a descriptive, speculative, historical science since it explains what is implicit in the present or past educational reality. [...] is normative, which aspires to verify its ideals in a subsequent activity. [...] Is practice or didactic art or ethics in action? (p.8)

Pedagogy is not only defined as science or technique or art or educational practice, but also as the norms that govern the entire educational process, for example Tomás Elias Zeitler (2010, p. 5) points out, "In the classrooms of the Brothers La Salle everything was strictly controlled, since every action or matter was attended to by the teacher: this was called the Pedagogy of Detail. Within this system of surveillance and control, silence was a matter of first order: communication through signals and sounds was considered to be essential within the classroom to maintain discipline and order."

Paulo Freire, the influential Brazilian writer, deserves a special mention. He develops themes about Pedagogy, treating them as an ideological and practical system in education, through his different works such as: Pedagogy of the oppressed (1994, Mexico), Pedagogy of autonomy (2010, Havana), Pedagogy of hope (1993, Mexico), Letters to those who intend to teach (1994, Mexico). Towards a Pedagogy of the Question (authored with Antonio Fernández, 1986, Argentina), in this last book (p.617) he points out that there is a Pedagogy of risk, a Pedagogy of error, and the Pedagogy of freedom or creation, putting Pedagogy before the response. Freire calls on us to promote education to achieve equality, transformation and inclusion of all individuals in society.

In summary, Pedagogy has gone through various theoretical sieves, through different perspectives, through many intellectual currents of pedagogues or not, each of them from their good intentions trying to contribute to its development, but, without intending to, generating a large number of concepts and opinions, sometimes contradictory, that give reason to Hugo Münsterberg when he points out the vagueness in pedagogical literature, and to A. de la Herrán, J. Paredes, C. Moral Santaella. and T. Muñoz (authors reviewed above) when they agree in pointing out the general ignorance of Spanish society about Pedagogy, and that it could extend to other societies.

To be fair to the different authors, it would be necessary to contextualize them in time, in the dominant thought of their time, the level of development of science and the epistemology that existed at that time. For example, Durkheim is currently cited a lot and based on what this illustrious sociologist points out, it is about establishing the concept of modern Pedagogy. Durkheim lived between 1858 and 1917. He is considered the initiator of sociology, so this discipline must have influenced his views on Pedagogy; epistemology had not been developed, therefore it did not have many auxiliary elements to discriminate the reflections of Durkheim. he. He was a promoter of structuralist functionalism which influenced him to propose his worldview of science and nature (social sciences must be holistic). Then Pedagogy went through a transition stage from art (practice) to theory (science), which was the object of analysis for Durkheim. Now, is Pedagogy at the beginning of the 20th century similar to Pedagogy in the 21st century? No, however, Durkheim's concept is valued, since it is useful in the construction process of Pedagogy, in its evolution, and because it is part of the heritage of his discursive system. But it would be a mistake, at the very least, not to question that concept. We should do this exercise for all great authors. Only in this way would we understand the logic of the evolution of Pedagogy in history.

2.2 ANALYSIS FOR THE RECONCEPTUATION OF PEDAGOGY

Given this conceptual tangle, it is valid to ask what Pedagogy really is? In the presence of modern authors who still require concepts that are somewhat debatable but have great roots, such as saying that Pedagogy is science, technique and art at the same time, we ask ourselves: Is it possible that Pedagogy is that? Is Pedagogy the science of education or is it part of the educational sciences or is it the great science of education that protects other educational sciences? Is Pedagogy a pansophy of education? These questions need to be answered with due rigor and foundation. It is an obligation of the members of the academic and teaching community to contribute with their research to clarify and justify the clearest definition of Pedagogy.

To contribute to the reconceptualization of Pedagogy, and try to rediscover the nature of Pedagogy, the following reflections and information are proposed from two different levels. In the foreground, the strategy of questions will be used to clarify certain conceptions of Pedagogy, and the substance of Pedagogy will also be analyzed from a logical and epistemological point of view, to define that essence with the greatest possible foundation.

a. *Is there a single epistemological position on the nature of Pedagogy?*

It is undoubtedly, due to the concepts of Pedagogy indicated above, that in the academic community, there are several epistemological positions regarding the nature of Pedagogy:

- Pedagogy as a philosophical theory of education.
- Pedagogy as a technique of education.
- Pedagogy as art or educational practice.
- Pedagogy as a science of education.
- Pedagogy as part of educational sciences.
- Pedagogy as Philosophy, science, Art of education.

If to these epistemological positions on Pedagogy, we add the socio-cultural meanings of the word Pedagogy (as a physical action of leading the child, as an educational practice, as a profession), we find a polysemic term, very misleading, a signifier with many meanings. This equivocation of the term goes contrary to the language of science itself, which requires a term to be monosemic, to be as univocal as possible. Scientific language is a hard language, whose vitality serves to avoid inaccuracies, ambiguities and conceptual errors. It is the obligation of the scientific community to reach a consensus to reduce the meanings and achieve as far as possible that for a signifier there is only one meaning. To a certain extent this would be one of the contributions of this work.

In principle, it must be noted that many of the indicated concepts were current in a historical space and time. Today, it is no longer accepted, for example, that Pedagogy has to do with physically or intellectually leading children. Nor is it accepted that Pedagogy is only and exclusively an educational practice or art. So the empirical evidence is decanting some conceptualizations of Pedagogy. However, positions still coexist that deny the scientific nature of Pedagogy, and accuse it of dealing only with the means, not with the ends or problems itself. They have reduced Pedagogy to a practice of transmitting knowledge, they have separated it from the possibility of using the scientific research process to investigate their own problems. This position considers Pedagogy as a technological discipline; therefore, it establishes the pedagogical process as different from the scientific process.

Some theorists who support the technological nature of Pedagogy, support their position by analyzing not the contents of Pedagogy but the pedagogical practice, which in reality are educational practices that constitute an educational fact. In reality, this is a confusion that arises from not distinguishing between educational practice where concepts, laws and theories are operated; and the discourse or pedagogical theory that should direct that practice. In other words, the two educational levels have not been differentiated: that of the facts of reality (educational practice), and that of pedagogical theories that are developed at a scientific level. R. Nassif (1958, p. 42) masterfully commented on it in the following way "that education is a doing, a practice, an activity; that, intentionally or not, shapes man. But from there to maintaining that Pedagogy is an activity, that is, an art, there is a great distance, because Pedagogy is not education, but the discipline that has it as its object." We should only consider this brilliant opinion of Nassif as such, one more opinion of the existing universe. A position that must be endorsed with the evidence of facts or reason.

In conclusion, even today there are several positions regarding the nature of Pedagogy, beyond those conceptualizations that are discarded due to their own empirical limitations.

b. Is there something common in all current epistemological positions?

Clearly yes. The issue where all intellectuals and pedagogues converge is that Pedagogy, whether defined as philosophy, science, technique or art, has as its object of study education as a human activity that must at least instruct and moralize. This is a good starting point, and the most important. Education, in general terms, constitutes the field of study of Pedagogy. Education is not speculation; it is not an illusion, it is a real fact contrasted by experience itself.

It is interesting to note that the Dictionary of the Royal Academy of the Spanish Language defines Pedagogy from two meanings: 1. f. Science that deals with education and teaching. 2. f. In general, what teaches and educates by doctrine or examples. The dictionary separates education and teaching, as if teaching were not part of the educational process. Teaching is a vital element of education, with it we instruct and moralize (they are the essential objectives of natural education), and teaching is an educational fact.

Education contains educational facts, which constitute actions, activities and educational processes. R. Bermúdez Sarguera, M Rodríguez Rebustillo. (2003, p. 20) explained:

For Leontiev in activity, the object with which the subject interacts, and the motive, coincide and are directed to satisfy a certain need. In actions, on the other hand, the object with which one interacts and the reason do not coincide. Actions are directed at objectives that are achieved sequentially to satisfy the final need that motivates the subject's activity..

Actions and activities are part of the educational process. If we wanted to relate to a larger field, or if education were located within a larger system, then we would indicate that educational processes are part of social processes. That is, education is one of many social processes. When reference is made to an educational fact, it should automatically refer to both those that correspond to natural education, which is generally an individual education, and those related to artificial education, which is generally an education of groups, of the masses.

c. Are educational facts studyable?

Educational facts are studyable, and can be done from different formalities and levels. From the empirical or vulgar level to the founded level. And the formalities (the cognitive formality that is part of grounded knowledge and involves the formal object, that is, the aspect under which reality is studied) would be: the technical, the scientific, the philosophical and the theological. Each formality generates a type of grounded knowledge.

Philosophical knowledge about education is theoretical, speculative or contemplative knowledge. Philosophical knowledge is concerned with identifying the nature of education, its purposes, its logic, its sources of knowledge, etc., all of this to find the most profound dissertation that reason can achieve about this natural or artificial process of humanity.

Scientific knowledge about education is knowledge generated by the use of the scientific method, whose purpose is to describe, explain and predict educational facts; using for this: concepts, categories, laws and theories. It is a testable knowledge (to verify or falsify reality), generally in monosemic, and representational language.

Technical knowledge about education is knowledge that describes, regulates, and standards the educational fact, for its transformation. It is the knowledge that applies other knowledge, scientific knowledge, to develop. It is knowledge constituted by a system of rules to improve doing, and action.

Theological knowledge about education describes the evolution of the educational fact from a religious vision, to lead man in his essence and existence towards the Supreme Being, divinity or absolute consciousness. This knowledge was called by Max Scheler the "knowledge of salvation."

d. Are there different types of knowledge or knowledge?

The answer to the previous question leads to admitting the existence of different types of knowledge. The mechanism that allows us to establish whether there are types of knowledge in the universe of knowledge begins with the selection of certain criteria that allow adequate differentiation based on the dominant and particular intrinsic characteristics of each branch of knowledge. For example, to differentiate the different biological species, we will not use criteria such as number of eyes or number of hearts, etc.; otherwise almost all living beings would be of the same species. More pertinent criteria, such as morphological or reproductive, would be used to carry out the classification. This same logic applies to every type of fact or phenomenon, such as the special case of education, where human talent is used in scientific, technical, artistic work, etc.; someone could dare to indicate that all educational knowledge They are artistic, since they all use imagination, skill and skills to infer non-analytical knowledge or why they all use that talent to generate knowledge.

For the purposes of our work, the criteria shown in Table No. 2 are being proposed. Based on these criteria, the classification mechanism requires identifying the particular and dominant characteristics of the knowledge or knowledge. The characteristics found define the nature of each discipline. In the case of our example, we will refer to the characteristics of philosophical, scientific, technological and artistic knowledge.

It is important to clarify that in each discipline there are some similar components, but the vast majority are different. Empirical evidence shows us that in nature and social life, there is no total identity between elements, only partial identities, and in the field of knowledge these partial identities are minimal and insubstantial. That is to say, although some elements may coincide with others (for example, the number of eyes in living beings), there are others that make us substantively different. And if that is true of knowledge, then we can establish the different "species" of knowledge.

Table Nº 2 Differences between philosophical, scientific, technological and artistic knowledge.

Criterion	Characteristics of Philosophy	Characteristics of Science	Technology Features	Characteristics of art
Purpose	The philosophy seems to identify the substance, the purposes, the logic, the sources of knowledge of reality, to find universal principles	Science seeks laws and theories to describe and explain reality	Technology seeks the production of things, to control and transform certain sectors of reality.	Art through its action seeks to satisfy the sensitivity of man
Content	They are theoretical, speculative or contemplative propositions, very general.	The body of knowledge contains hypo-deductive propositions; it generates specific representational knowledge.	The body of knowledge is normative, regulatory propositions, operational knowledge.	It is a type of action, or a special product outside the rigidity of logical laws.
Type of problem addressed	Metaphysical problem and linguistic problems	Cognitive problems about concrete/abstract natural and social phenomena	Practical problems referring to artificial and concrete facts	Aesthetics
Final product	Rational and critical knowledge, which involves uncertainty and doubt	Knowledge. The relative truth of knowledge is an end and a means	Artifacts, action plan, things or objects. The truth is a means.	A painting, a sculpture, a poem, the exposition of a speech, etc.
Evaluation criterion	Rational or irrational	Knowledge subject to ethical evaluation (true or false)	Artifacts or objects subject to efficiency and effectiveness criteria.	Actions or products subject to the criteria of beauty, pleasantness
Social impact	Philosophy is not harmful to society	Science is not harmful to society.	The technique can be beneficial or harmful to society.	Art has a very limited effect on society
Type of good produced	cultural asset	Generally it is a cultural and public good	It is a cultural asset and it is always a commodity.	It is a cultural asset and only its products are a commodity.
Research method	M. Rational, M. Dialectic, M. Hermeneutic	M. of Scientific Research	M. of technological research	Practice and talent
Way of approaching the investigation	Questions that remain open and without definitive solutions.	Problem, hypothesis, contrast hypotheses	Problem-need, select solution, experiment, develop the artifact, evaluate it	Spontaneous
Dominant process	Rational and critical	Analytical	Synthetic	Creative
Workspace	Your own being	Generally in scientific laboratories	Generally in the field and industrial laboratories.	Your workshop or your space of expression

This information should help define whether the dominant body of knowledge of a discipline fits the nature of any of them.

e. Is basic science the same as applied science? Is applied science the same as technology?

Considering the current importance of scientific knowledge and its complexity, and given the confusion that exists when identifying What is it? Of basic-applied sciences-technology, certain differences are detailed:

What is basic science? They are knowledge generated by the use of the scientific method whose purpose is to satisfactorily describe and explain different phenomena of reality, regardless of their possible practical use.

What is applied science? They are knowledge generated by the use of the scientific method whose purpose is to satisfactorily describe and explain different phenomena of reality in search of their possible practical use. Applied science can be defined as the set of applications of basic (or pure) science to know the probable uses of certain concepts or theories.

What is the difference between basic and applied science? To answer this question, a couple of examples from Mario Bunge (1984, pp. 34-35) will be used, which will help us understand the difference:

Those who study the flora of a country do botany and those who investigate plant resources do applied botany: they search for and study plants, trees or fungi of possible use in food, medicine or industry. Applied botanists do not deal with the process of transforming plants into food, drugs or construction materials; this is non-scientific technical matter. Applied botanists are scientists who, instead of dealing with basic and general problems, such as genetics, evolution or physiology, use basic knowledge to individualize, classify, describe and analyze plant species of possible practical use. It is clear that, in the course of his research, the applied botanist will be able to make discoveries of interest to basic science; For example, he may discover species or varieties characterized by an abnormal number of chromosomes or by self-regulation mechanisms not used by others.

In any case, the applied scientist uses the same method as the basic scientist. The difference is that both apply the scientific method to different types of problems. In summary, both basic and applied research uses the scientific method to obtain new knowledge (data, hypotheses, theories, calculation or measurement techniques, etc.). But while the basic researcher works on the problems that interest him (for purely cognitive reasons), the applied researcher studies problems of possible social interest. Hence, while applied research can be planned in the long term, basic research cannot.

What are the differences between science and technology? We continue using the example of Mario Bunge (1984, pp. 35-36),

Here is a physicist who studies the interactions between light and electrons, in particular the photoelectric effect, (photovoltaics). This person does basic science, whether theoretical or experimental, if the only goal is to enrich human knowledge of the interactions between light and matter. In the adjacent laboratory, another physicist studies the photoelectric activity of certain particularly sensitive substances, in order to better understand how photoelectric cells work, which in turn could be used to make more efficient photoelectric devices. This researcher does applied science (theoretical or experimental) because he applies knowledge obtained in basic research. Of course, it is not limited to applying existing knowledge: far from that, it seeks new knowledge, but more special ones, since they do not refer to the interaction of light and matter in general, but between light of certain colors and matter of certain colors classes.

Let us now move from scientific to industrial laboratories. The industrial laboratory does not produce knowledge but rather technology: it is, as Sábato says, a technology factory. For example, in it

we may also find a researcher who studies photoelectric cells, but not only to know how they work, but to design a battery of photo-voltaic cells to power a house. This person is not a scientist but an engineer (high-level, of course) and, as such, his sights are set on useful artifacts. For him, science is not an end but a means.

Finally, let's move from the research and development laboratory to a factory that manufactures on a commercial scale the photo-voltaic cell batteries designed by our engineer. The purpose of this activity is different from that which animated the activities of the scientist or engineer: now it is about obtaining profits either for the shareholders of the company or for society. Not even the artifact that was a goal for the engineer is now a goal; If its marketing is not profitable, the company's leaders will order their technicians to design devices of another type. This is clear and yet many experts continue to confuse industrial products, or services, with scientific products.

Distinguishing types of activity does not imply separating them. We all know that what begins as disinterested research can end up as a commodity (eg a television) or a service (eg a medical treatment).

So, according to Bunge (to which the author belongs), there are differences between Applied Science and Technology. The difference between them is defined not only by the example cited, but by the differences that the author proposes in table No. 1. Emphasizing that one of the inputs of Technology to fulfill its functions is Science (among them Applied).

In the modern era, unlike all previous eras, there is an incessant flow from basic to applied research, from the former to technology, and from the latter to the economy (production, marketing and services), so that B. Latour (1992, p. 29) for this reason, when visualizing this exchange when studying the activity of scientists and engineers, introduced the concept of technoscience. In Cuba J. Nuñez (1999) promoted the term "technoscience", the same as A. Adúriz Bravo (2001, p. 287, to refer to Didactics) in Spain. But, for Mario Bunge (2009, p. 73), far from referring to that term as a neologism describing a certain reality, he considered "technoscience" as a conceptual scam, when he noted: "these disastrous experiences serve to warn against the confusion that hides the barbarism 'technoscience', fashionable among sociologists of knowledge who do not know how to distinguish science from technique." Along the same lines, I. Niiniluoto (1997) states that the use of the term Technoscience, used especially by sociologists of science, is inadequate, since it wastes and disturbs the characteristics of both.

f. Can Pedagogy or any other branch of knowledge be made up of knowledge of a different nature? That is, can Pedagogy be science, technology and art at the same time?

Definitely not. The foundation of this assertion is based on the use of common sense, Euler/Venn diagrams, the laws of logic, information theory and everyday empirical evidence, which are detailed below. But, advancing an argument for didactic purposes, we will point out the following: any branch of knowledge, whether philosophical or scientific or technological, the number of propositions inherent to its nature should constitute 90% of its cognitive domain, incorporating 10% of other types. of propositions (the figures are not supported by empirical evidence, they only serve to graph a reality). As research is carried out, for example in science, concepts and categories of philosophical knowledge can be developed. But this does not mean that because of these concepts found, Science becomes Philosophy. This phenomenon confirms the premises that "nothing is absolutely pure" and that "every rule has its exception." For the purposes of classifying the nature of a branch of knowledge, the dominant or most numerous propositions are used.

Let's first identify the source of the confusion, I think that the problem is one of perspective: Concluding that Pedagogy is science, technique and art, is given by the way in which the educational fact is approached. First, we must admit that the educational fact is complex and unitary. As such, in the educational event all the ingredients are present (art, science and technique), so analyzing its different dimensions with a single conceptual tool leads to error. Therefore, studying the educational process as a "black box" does not allow us to differentiate the components. That is, the educational fact is studied as a whole, as if it were a single structure without compartments or elements. The whole is perceived, without differentiating the interrelated parts. It is not "understood" that each component of the educational event can be clearly differentiated with its own nature and function, without the need to separate them in the process. Therefore, whoever follows this perspective has not differentiated between what the discipline per se (Pedagogy) is, with the exercise of that discipline (art or educational practice). They do not know how to differentiate between the nature of things and the way in which the thing is applied or operates.

In this confusion of perspective, it is not understood that what is interesting to study or characterize is the discipline in all its dimensions, and not the way in which it could operate, nor who does it. The first intention is in the field of knowledge, and the other is in the operational field. What is important to define for our purposes is what is (Pedagogy)? And not how to do it? It is obvious that in the educational task, the protagonist (generally the teacher) combines all the resources available to him: science, technique and art. It is in the person where all these characteristics come together. But in reality, there are things of a different nature that come together in it. He uses pedagogical and other science theories and laws, not as teaching content, but to understand and develop his educational process (science of education); he uses educational strategies, media and materials to make his process more efficient (educational technology); He also puts his energy, style, talent to contribute to the effective development of the process (art of education).

An example could clarify us: Let's imagine a good carpenter (a simile of the good teacher), he has in his workshop hammers (philosophical knowledge), saws (scientific knowledge), chisels (technological knowledge), nails (other types of knowledge), but he also has their talent (art or the teacher's educational practice). To do a good work (carry out a good training process), first, you must understand that each instrument (knowledge) is different, has a different nature and therefore fulfills different functions. Second, accept that each instrument is generated by different factories or goldsmiths (to be able to acquire it if necessary). Third, distinguishing each instrument must be used according to the demands of each activity. There is only one work, but different instruments are used that complement and interact due to the carpenter's ability. The important thing is that he knows how to distinguish them, otherwise he would use the hammer to cut wood.

i. Let's use Common Sense to define if it is possible for a branch of knowledge to have three different natures.

Why would it be a mistake to accept a concept whose meaning encompasses the universe of its signifiers, or a "thing" is three or four things of different nature at the same time, such as concluding that Pedagogy is science, philosophy, art and technology? At the same time?

To admit that Pedagogy is several things at the same time: art, technique and science, is to admit a fact that has no correlation with everyday, natural and cultural experience if things are analyzed within a single reference system, that is, in the same circumstances and conditions. To illustrate this, let's use three experiences:

First experience: Can a single element have three types of manifestations? YEAH. Take water as an example: it manifests itself in liquid, gaseous and solid states. However, for this to happen we must agree that although appearances are different, the nuclear, molecular structure of water does not change, it is the same. Different manifestations, but the same essence, the same nature.

With this we conclude that essentially, science, technology and art are the same in their nuclear structure. Is this so? Table No. 2 shown above gives the answer. It shows that art, science and technology do not have the same basic structure. They are substantially different. Therefore, this experience does not apply to justify the claim that Pedagogy is three or four things at the same time.

Second experience. Can water be oil and mercury at the same time in the same space–time? That is, can a substance be at the same time another substance(s) of a different structure or nature? Ontologically, if a thing is a substance it cannot be another substance in the same space-time. Undoubtedly, reality and logic tell us that this is neither possible nor probable. Taking it to the level of knowledge, one could say: that a law is scientific or it is not scientific, but stating that a law is scientific, technological and artistic at the same time subjects us to a well-founded questioning. A scientific law, which is based on certain philosophical assumptions and applied in vast technological fields, is easier to understand and accept. Therefore, this experience shows us the impossibility of one thing having three different natures in the same historical space-time.

Third experience, Let's see, can God be spirit and matter at the same time? For religious Christians: God is Spirit. His own condition as a deity would prevent him from having a material constitution, to the extent that matter has many limitations and that would be consistent with his divinity.

Surely some religious people will wonder: Jesus as God made man? In principle Jesus was the Son of God. He lost his divine quality when he became man, with all his limitations inherent to that nature. Some others will say, what about the Holy Trinity, three persons in one God? Although this is not a treatise on Theology, we will say that this teaching is a mystery; mystery that we will try to unravel. First, biblically it is taught that God is the Father and not that he is made up of three different persons (by the way, the Holy Spirit is not a person and is represented as a dove or flame of fire). Even if we accept that the Trinity exists, let us use the following earthly metaphor to understand: God would be a research management corporation, composed of representatives of the government (resembling the Father), representatives of the Universities (resembling the son), and the company representatives (resembles the Holy Spirit). In any case, God is not father, nor son, nor holy spirit at the same time (This was visualized at the time of Jesus' baptism: The son was baptized, the spirit was another different being (a dove) and the Father who spoke from the heavens. If the deity with all his omniscience and omnipresence finds it "difficult" to have that triple nature, let us imagine any human creation, including a branch of knowledge.

ii. From the point of view of the laws of logic.

JuanAmós Comenio (1998, p. 81), in his masterpiece Didactica Magna, chapter XXI, Method of the Arts, section 10, used this line of argument that we propose, saying "The same thing in Logic, that dilemma: either it is day , or at night, so it is night, therefore it is not day, can be easily imitated with all the opposite contrary propositions of the aforementioned manner. For example: Either he is uncultured or learned, so he is uncultured. Therefore he is not learned; Cain was pious or he was impious, so he was not pious, then..., etc."Applying the laws of logic can help us resolve this issue, given that logical laws, by their nature, avoid confusion and contradiction. Whether it is philosophy or it is technique; It is either science or art; they cannot be both together.

Using the four laws or principles of logic: the principle of identity, contradiction, excluded third and sufficient reason, the nature of pedagogy will be established:

1. The identity principle. It tells us that a thing is identical to itself, what it is, is; What is not, it is not:

$$A \text{ is } A, \text{ or not } A \text{ is not } A,$$

Applying it to our case, if we begin by conceptualizing Pedagogy as a science that contains the other disciplines (for the purposes of analysis, it could begin by saying that it is a philosophical theory or an art, etc., that contains the others):

C: Science, set of testable propositions.
 F: Philosophy, set of non-testable propositions.
 T: Technology, set of regulatory propositions.
 A: Art, a set of descriptive, non-regulatory propositions.
 Q: Pedagogy

So.

If P is C: and, C is C, then P is C.
 If P is C; and, C is not F; So P is not F.
 If P is C; and, C is not T; So P is not T.
 If P is C; and, C is not A, then; P is not A.

Conclusion: if Pedagogy is science then it is not Philosophy, it is not Technology, it is not Art. Admitting that science is a system of hypo-deductive propositions subjected to the rigor of logic, and Art is more of an activity, and whose descriptive formulations are not subject at all to laws of logic, then it is clear that they are of a different nature. This analysis demonstrates, for example, that stating that there is a "science that is also an art" is a contradiction, which does not conform to this law. Since a hypo-deductive system of propositions does not contain, nor is it, any type of activity.

The same analysis could be carried out if we begin by conceptualizing Pedagogy as Technology, or as Philosophical Theories or as Art. The conclusions are the same, it is impossible for a discipline to contain the entire universe of propositions. So, if Pedagogy is science, it cannot be Technology, Philosophy or an Art.

2. The principle of contradiction. It tells us that it is impossible to affirm and deny that a thing is and is not at the same time and under the same circumstance. Or, it can also be stated that two contradictory propositions cannot be true at the same time.

$$A \text{ is not not } A$$

For our purposes it is easier to apply this law:

1. The same conditions follow for C, F, T, A, and P.
2. If we use C as a reference (science, it could start with anyone).
3. If we accept the differences in the nature of different knowledge,

So:

F is not C

T is not C

A is not C

So; C is not F

C is not T

C is not A

And, if P is C; so
    P is not F
    P is not T
    ....P is not A.

In conclusion, if we admit that Pedagogy is science, then we must reject that Pedagogy is Philosophical theory or Technology or Art.

1. **The principle of excluded middle.** It tells us that a thing is or is not, there is no middle ground. Or, it can also be stated that there is no middle between two contradictory propositions.

A is B, or A is not B.

As the statement of this logical law says, there are no middle terms, either Pedagogy is science or Pedagogy is not science. Pedagogy is technology or Pedagogy is not technology. There are no middle terms. It is not that it is a techno-science or any other type. As M Bunge would say, classifying Pedagogy as Technoscience is barbaric because it ignores the difference between these disciplines.

The final conclusion of applying these laws, Pedagogy constitutes solely and exclusively a branch of knowledge. Either it is science, or it is Technology, or it is Philosophical Theory or it is Art, there is no longer any room for the unfounded pretension of establishing a hyper hybrid nature of Pedagogy. We would like to make a preview that will be discussed in the next chapter. These laws of logic can be applied to define whether the assertion that "Didactics is science, technology and art" is true or false, to admit that Didactics has a single nature.

From the point of view of scientific rigor, the minimum required is that its statements (concepts) be consistent, not contradictory, since this reduces their veracity or explanatory capacity. The effect of an inconsistency or falsity in part of a theory, applying standard logic, would be to jeopardize the entire theory. If we are careful about our own scientific work, we must be very careful in exposing or accepting statements without having proven their consistency and veracity.

iii. From the point of view of information theory

As an addition to all the arguments presented, one related to information theory will be added. First, a premise of Claude Shannon's Information Theory is established. R. Antonio, L. Castro, and RJ Fusario (1999, p. 264), pointed out:

Information is a set of data that allows us to clarify something about what is unknown to us. [...] An event that is known for certain to occur does not contain any information. Therefore, an event will contain a greater amount of information the lower its probability of occurrence. [...] We can assume that each message may have an associated probability of occurrence, such that the greater the probability that this message is true, the less information it contains for the user..

From these premises,L. Piscoya (1974, p. 29) expresses:

Any formulation that includes every possibility without ruling out any is an empty message. We will illustrate this statement with an example: suppose that a person who asks a doctor about the health of a sick person receives the response "my opinion is that the sick person will be cured or he will not be cured." In this case, the doctor's response will not provide the questioner with any information about the patient because it is a statement that logically is a complete disjunction, that is, it includes all the possibilities that can arise in the situation in question.

Obviously, in order to report something, the doctor would have to select one of the options and discard the other. Consequently, a definition [...] that says that this can be everything, that is, that it includes all the possibilities of the universe of discourse, suffers from a serious methodological flaw, since it does not provide any information and is as Byzantine as the doctor's response. from our example.

These quotes tell us that a concept that contains the entire universe of signifiers is a concept that does not provide real information; Its all-encompassing meaning, instead of becoming a virtue, results in a horrible defect.

iv. From the point of view of Mathematics

Now we will reinforce information theory using the Euler/Venn diagram. Mathematics, as an auxiliary discipline to other disciplines, has served as an important support to specify and clarify its propositions, whatever their nature. Let's use the diagrams to graph the arguments.

Be:

C: Set of testable propositions (scientific)
F: Set of non-contrastable propositions, (philosophical)

T: Set of regulative propositions (technology)
A: Set of descriptive, non-regulatory (artistic) propositions.

U: Universal set, it would be all knowledge about education.

C = P (Pedagogy): body of scientific knowledge about education.
No P: Set of other knowledge.

In its relationship with Pedagogy, it would be: P = U - No P

To graph the properties of the sets, Figure No. 1 will be used.

Fig. No. 1 Types of knowledge in Education.

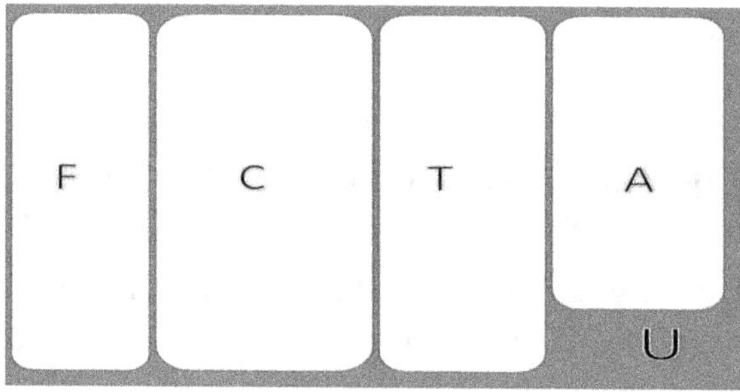

The figure shows the existence of four subsets, which represent philosophical, scientific, technological and artistic knowledge. They are subsets with totally different elements, totally independent, without anything that relates them, inscribed in the Universal set. To complete the Universe, theological and empirical knowledge would be lacking. In this reductionist synthesis, C (pedagogy) is only a subset, different but interrelated with other knowledge about education; they are knowledge that complement each other to give meaning to the educational fact.

Finally, experience and life itself show us that there is nothing that contains everything at the same time and in the same space, that is absolute. Life teaches us to distrust things that are seen as panaceas. The same must happen with those branches of knowledge that are constituted as pansophies, which know or encompass everything. All-embracing things only exist in desire.

Some have pointed out that Medicine is similar to Pedagogy, and therefore contains all types of knowledge propositions. In reality, Medicine is not the same as Pedagogy, rather, its simile would be Education. Just like this, it can be studied from different levels, so that there are medical knowledge that is scientific (Anatomy, Physiology, Neurophysiology, etc.), other technological (protocols for open heart surgery, etc.), other artistic (acting styles that reduce aesthetic impacts), other philosophical ones (causal or ecological models to address health, definition of illness, life, etc.). It is the doctor, just like the teacher, who develops or uses all this knowledge.

After all the arguments presented, from our perspective, there is no doubt that the concepts of Pedagogy that give it an all-embracing character do not adjust to logical and epistemological analysis. Believing otherwise implies contracting an "intellectual disease." Miguel A. Zabalza Beraza (2007), referring to the all-embracing nature of Didactics, describes it like this (I highlight the idea of intellectual illness in bold):

We began the previous point by pointing out that University Didactics was, in the usual manuals, "the science and art of teaching." But it is a somewhat schizophrenic definition and less explanatory than it should be. What is teaching and its knowledge, an art or a science? Can an activity be science and art at the same time? [...] It may seem like a banal issue or a topic of discussion for opposing candidates. But it's not like that. It is a key issue because depending on the position adopted, our actions as teachers

> *will have a sufficiently stable and predictable character on the one hand (science) or they will appear as activities dependent on the situation, personal style or the particular circumstances that occur at that time. moment (art). In the same way, if everything depends on the will and expertise of each person (art), there is little room for systematic knowledge and a discipline like Didactics would have little to contribute (pp. 494, 495)*

Rather, we must accept that there are propositions of different types, which belong to different branches of knowledge. These propositions are basically contained in a specific body of knowledge. This knowledge is generated by research in certain disciplines. Now, for argumentative propositions without measurement requirements that explain the physical and metaphysical world of education, there is a specific discipline that is Educational Philosophy. For hypo-deductive propositions that build formal or empirical theories, there is the discipline that is the Science of Education. For regulative propositions that constitute a system of rules and procedures to improve an action, there is a specific discipline which is Educational Technology.

g. Why identify Pedagogy with the science(s) that Education studies, and what is required for this?

It could have started by discriminating the type of proposition that corresponds to Pedagogy, and then identifying its real nature. But we will take the shortest and most agreed upon shortcut, of identifying Pedagogy with the Science of Education for two reasons: the first, because it is almost a consensus in the community of theorists associated with education that Pedagogy is a science (beyond of the discussion if it is a science or if it is the sciences, which will be analyzed later, or if it is a science + technique + art, since they put the character of science first). And second, because following Henri Marion's reasoning in Ferdinand Buisson's Dictionnaire de pédagogie (1887), when he pointed out that:

> *Pedagogy is (...) the science and art of education. But since it is necessary to choose, since in our language the use of the same word to simultaneously designate an art and the corresponding science is frowned upon, I will not hesitate to define Pedagogy simply: the science of education. Why science before art? Because (...) the substance of Pedagogy does not reside in the methods it uses, but rather in the theoretical reasons by which it finds those methods, judges them and coordinates them.*

AND The author accepts the position that Pedagogy is a science.

For many historians of education, Herbart is the first to try to provide Pedagogy with a scientific foundation. With it, pedagogy leaves its primary, empirical and operational state and acquires the level of analytical, theoretical and systematic knowledge. Pedagogy as a science was developed with the development of the human sciences, in the desire of its promoters to give a higher level of rigor to all its propositions. With these preliminary considerations, it is vital to establish the conditions that must be met by a discipline that would like to have scientific status. The acceptance of Pedagogy as a science (or sciences) implies that it is not necessary to demonstrate that the pedagogical theoretical system is hypo-deductive, that its propositions are demonstrative, representational, and that its knowledge meets all the standards of scientific knowledge. Thus, other elements that are required of a discipline to achieve the status of science will be analyzed. What are these?

J. Tusquets (1969, p.76) pointed out that what fundamentally justifies a science is its method. For him, Comparative Pedagogy is "the science that raises and attempts to solve educational problems using the comparative method [...] Comparative Pedagogy is substantially a method. "Questioning or denying it, as Schneider does, seems to me to make things crazy." It is justified that the existence of a method can create a discipline, therefore a comparative science can exist.

C. Álvarez de Zayas (2004, p. 32), referring to Didactics, mentioned "Didactics is a science because it has its own object of study that identifies it as such and also its own methodology."

Is it enough to have an object of study, some methods to convert a body of knowledge into autonomous science? No, it is not enough, in our opinion. The mere apparent identification of the object of study is not a guarantee of anything. For example, philosophy, technologies and techniques have objects of study, special methods, and this does not make them sciences.

For these reasons, the proposals of Álvarez de Zayas and Tusquets are insufficient. Popper states that what distinguishes a discipline is not so much its object of study (almost always shared), but the type of problems it helps to solve (taken from D. Antiseri, 1977, p. 476).M. Bunge (1999, pp. 27 – 31) points out that to identify a science, a conceptual, empirical, historical and social aspect must be considered. To define what science is, there must exist a scientific community, where its members agree or not with all ideas but communicate with each other. Clarity in the philosophical assumptions that direct the research work of its members. There must be a domain or universe of discourse, namely, the set of facts or ideas that the scientific community in question studies. A formal background: the use of logical discourse rules for the construction of discourse. A specific background, the theories of other sciences that support the construction of the science analyzed. An accumulated fund of knowledge of that science in question. The problem or set of problems addressable by science. The objectives of science and methodology (collection of methods). In short, we understand that identifying the scientific status of a discipline is a more complex issue than simply requiring the definition of an object of study and a methodology.

Another great epistemologist, Stephen Toulmin (1972), establishes the following characteristics for a discipline to be considered scientific: It must contain a set of specific conceptual or practical problems (similar to the Problematics proposed by Bunge); exist a critical professional community; must have a general and shared point of view about the discipline (similar to philosophical assumptions); must have accepted strategies and procedures (similar to methodical); and finally it must contain evolving conceptual populations linked to specific problems (similar to Bunge's accumulated fund).

Not analyzing Pedagogy with this requirement of prerequisites can result in a dangerous reductionism, and a deficient epistemological study. But not only that: in addition to the aforementioned, there are certain conditions that a discipline must meet to be considered scientific. One of them is that it should not be isolated. That is, all science is part of a system of sciences. That is, each science has some neighboring science with which it overlaps, even partially. For example, in the case of physics and chemistry, the overlap is physical chemistry. Biology and physics combine to form biophysics, and so on.

If Pedagogy is a (social) science, what is its object of study? In a broad sense its object is education; In a strict sense, the educational facts that involve the interaction of people (teachers-students-society), policies, organization, culture and the genetic and neurophysiological structure of the actors, with a certain purpose. Therefore, its propositions that describe and explain those facts must be testable in objective reality. Although the existence of a perceived reality is admitted, it does not serve to contrast propositions, it is only a space for interpretation by the knowing subject. Its specific background is the contribution of Sociology, Psychology, Economics, Statistics, etc., which by having a field of study in education generate information that is useful to Pedagogy.

b. Does science constitute itself as it matures spontaneously or does it have phases of development? What state or phase is it in?

Pedagogy participates in a fundamental characteristic of all science, that of being a permanent, dialectical construction, in search of new problems that guide its research. Pedagogy, more than any other science, is not closed or finished knowledge, but rather an open system of concepts with many points of contact with other disciplines or sciences and little by little it consolidates a theoretical system that is its own. There is no science that is definitive or with absolute knowledge about its object.

The pedagogical discourse – like that of any other science – is in full construction. From our perspective, it is just being formed as a theoretical system, because it is based on specific theories of certain sciences, such as psychology or sociology. According to Foucault (1972, pp. 313-314), "scientificity" has various modalities or thresholds:

"With regard to a discursive formation, several different emergencies can be described. The moment from which a discursive practice is individualized and acquires its autonomy, the moment, therefore, in which a single system of formation of statements is operating, or also the moment in which this system is transformed, can be called the threshold of positivity.

When in the game of a discursive formation, a set of statements is cut short, it attempts to enforce (even without achieving) norms of verification and coherence and exercises, with respect to knowledge, a dominant function (of model, criticism or verification) it will be said that discursive formation crosses a threshold of epistemologization.

When the epistemological figure thus drawn obeys a certain number of formal criteria, when its statements do not only respond to archaeological rules of formation, but also to certain laws of construction of propositions, it will be said that it has crossed a threshold of scientificity.

In short, when scientific discourse in turn can define the axioms that are necessary to it, the elements that it uses, the propositional structures that are legitimate for it and the transformations that it accepts when it can thus deploy, from itself, the formal edifice that constitutes, it will be said that it has crossed the threshold of formalization

We must keep in mind that a science goes through various phases of development until it reaches a moment in which it definitively acquires its scientific status, since the sciences appear in the element of a discursive formation and on a background of knowledge. Specifically, Pedagogy, as a discursive formation, as a scientific discipline, has already emerged positively; "It works in the element of knowledge" and has therefore crossed the threshold of positivity.

He crossed the threshold of epistemologization, when his theories and laws are evaluated, classified, validated from within himself, with the criteria emanating from within, as he identified his object and operated with criteria of scientific research, working on his models of discovery and validation. Pedagogy is moving to the level of scientificity, building its own laws and theories, many of which are questioned and others accepted by small groups of pedagogues and many others in reconstruction, making them more measurable so that they comply with the "requirements of a scientific law." " (E. Hashimoto. 2006). An example of a pedagogical law is described in this work (p. 110), the product of a research work that used the research method advocated by the work, and which was made available to the scientific community of Peru, and proposes: **"In almost all cases where a people training process is carried out, when there is a favorable relationship of will between the teacher and the learner, the learning of the latter will be significant and of better quality.**

Another element of analysis to establish the character of mature science of pedagogy is Stephen Toulmin's (1972) classification, whose criterion is the fulfillment of the characteristics that a discipline must possess to be scientific. Disciplines can be: compact or mature. (they meet all the characteristics); the diffuse ones (they fulfill some of them) and the possible ones (when they can bring them together).

From this perspective, too, Pedagogy is not yet an epistemologically mature science, it is an emerging science, it has not gone through a rigorous logical and epistemological analysis of its theoretical system: laws and theories, to differentiate between them, the axiomatic and semantic structure of their proposals.

As Pedagogy concretizes its own elements that identify it as a science, it has gone from its technical conception, which history forged, to becoming an emerging science, a condition in which it must be studied in all educational centers. Emerging, not in the semantic sense, but in the Foucauldian sense, where "Pedagogy" historically struggled with the technical and art conception that dominated since Greek times. According to J. Marshall (1994, p. 23) points out:

> *The concept of emergency considers the present, not in a finalist sense, as a result of historical evolution, but rather as a stage in the war process of confrontation between opposing forces in search of*

*control and domination.[...] We do not consider, therefore, ,
historical "developments" as culminations of historical processes,
intentions of great actors or hidden political designs, but as manifestations of the balances of power over people.*

Pedagogical analysis must take into account this intertwining of education with historical events. We believe that Pedagogy must be studied as a discipline that continues in the attempt to formalize itself as a science, to the extent that it tries to axiomatize the complex phenomenon of education. The reference to history is not for the purpose of accumulating foreign knowledge unrelated to the current situation of educational practice, nor is it the tendency to naively take tradition as a norm of action for the future. Because it is evident that currently the pedagogical discourse constituted with a more or less established scientific status that can be identified, has been taking shape little by little until acquiring its specific character alongside other consolidated scientific discourses.

It is vital to continue with the logical analysis of the pedagogical propositions to formalize each one of them. For this reason, it is stated that Pedagogy has not crossed the threshold of formalization. But, it must be noted that each discursive formation does not successively pass through these different thresholds as if they were the natural stages of biological maturation.

However, understanding this lack of maturity of Pedagogy as a scientific discipline is useful to recognize the need to strengthen with methodological and epistemological rigor all the propositions that are formulated as laws or pedagogical theories; Furthermore, to understand why the open debate generated for more than a century continues on the singular or plural character of Pedagogy as a science: Is Pedagogy a science of education or educational sciences? This dilemma is not a matter of semantics or a matter of quantity; it is a problem of epistemological perspectives.

i. Educational science or educational sciences: Which position has greater epistemological status?

A little history seems pertinent to us. Marc-Antoine Julien (called "from Paris"), from 1801 to 1819, dedicated himself entirely to educational issues, writing several works, including Essai général d'éducation in 1808. In 1810 he studied at the Pestalozzi Institute. It was like a revelation: for 3 months he lived with the Swiss pedagogue in Yverdon with his wife and children. He maintained a permanent correspondence with Pestalozzi, to whom he entrusted the education of his children. There he conceived the "sciences of education." After spending two years in prison and a new stay at the Institute, he began to spread the theories of Pestalozzi and Fellenberg in France and published in the Journal d'éducation, which he had helped to found, "Letters on the method of education of Mr. Pestalozzi" and, above all, in 1817, the work of comparative education that made him famous [...]. He then broke with Pestalozzi and called him a traitor [...] With Jullien, the science of education became comparativist. (Jacqueline Gautherin. 1999).

L. García Aretio (1989, p. 53) reminds us that "On October 21, 1912, the JJ Roousseau Institute of Educational Sciences was created in Geneva," to promote the training of teachers in experimental and psychological pedagogy. For children, and stimulate the development of Pedagogy. Francine Best (1988, p. 163) goes on to note:

> Gaston Mialaret, who had directed with Maurice Debesse a Traité des sciences pédagogiques (1971) and who wanted to remove Pedagogy from its ambiguous and non-scientific situation, took the term "educational sciences" from Switzerland, where it operated at the University of Geneva. A chair so called. Of course, this loan clarifies the question of the scientific condition and turns education into an object of knowledge, but the plural adopted is very signifi-

cant: the educational sciences are nothing more than a part of the social sciences that already had a certain reputation. academic. It is about the psychology of education, the sociology of education, and the history of education. This new formula distances us from the equation adopted by Mario and Buisson: "Pedagogy (...) is the science of education."

In 1967, in France the concept of "Educational Sciences" was consolidated, with the creation, in universities, of an Educational Sciences study program in the Faculties of Letters.

Just as in France all attempts related to the autonomy, disciplinarization and institutionalization of Pedagogy in university spaces were discredited and occupied a secondary place, precisely because their teaching was added most of the time to the teaching of philosophy. , of psychology (in the case of Foucault) or of sociology (in the case of Espinas, of Durkheim)'; also, in Geneva some attempts to energize Pedagogy and provide it with a new orientation were displaced." (R. Ríos Beltrán (s/a p. 4).

France being the cradle of this proposal, has kept the flame of this debate alive, G. Avanzini (1982, p. 119) describes that "There is no Congress, a meeting in Educational Sciences where the problem of the specificity of our discipline not be raised.

In England (the same in English-speaking countries), for semantic reasons, they do not express themselves using the concept of Pedagogy, because it practically does not exist, but Educational Sciences, because it is within their common and scientific vocabulary, which is why the concept of Educational Sciences has been easier to accept and propagate, both in their English-speaking societies and in the societies that are influenced by them.

This helps us understand why in the Anglo-Saxon world and its satellites, the science of education is not related to Pedagogy. But, in the case of the French it is really strange, since there are excellent intellectuals who are in permanent debate. Why don't the French accept that Pedagogy is the science of education? Let's try some reasons:

- The first reason comes from the lack of rigor with which specialists in the subject handled the meanings of the word Pedagogy. This is reflected in the equivocation or polysemy described above. Debesse's argument (1976, p. 71) paints this argument in full: "If I proposed and obtained the use of the expression educational sciences at the level of university education, rather than talking about Pedagogy, it has not been because to detest this old word or to substitute for it, by a ridiculous usurpation, a more dazzling title. It is because the word pedagogy has become doubly wrong at the same time that it is too limiting and at the same time too imprecise."On this matter Agustín Escolano (1978, p. 21-22) stated that:

At the same time that the expression "educational sciences" comes to mean an alleged positivity, it is worth not forgetting that the abolition of the term "Pedagogy" also responds to the limiting and imprecise meaning of this last name", restrictions that have been marked, among other authors by Deesse (1973), Clausse (1970), Mialaret (1973), Ferry (1967) and Faure (1973), and which could be summarized in the following observations: Limitations derived from the etymology of the term Pedagogy, which in the sense Strictly speaking, it would only include studies on childhood education. Reduction in scope to the narrow circle of the internal concerns of traditional Pedagogy. Possible didactic-practical identification of pedagogical works.

The big problem was that specialists, whether pedagogues or not, developed new meanings for Pedagogy, due to historical-cultural demands, but did not rigorously provide the corresponding foundations why the previous meanings were inadequate or had limitations. They did not substantiate the conceptualizations, and only expressed their good intentions of what Pedagogy should be like.

- The second reason has to do with the operationalization of the concept and the hierarchy of educational work. The French historically related, quite rightly, Pedagogy to the application of the theories and laws that consolidated sciences such as sociology and psychology could provide. It was a "practical science." Therefore, at that time competing with an explanatory and predictive science that the other social sciences had would have been a mistake. In those historical moments, the pretension of Pedagogy, without its own theories and laws to support it as a science, must have hurt the susceptibility of French intellectuals. Francine Best, Maurice Debesse and others (1972, p. 58) summarized it this way, "the word Pedagogy does not sound good to the French. "He was used with a certain repugnance." Else:

Emile Durkheim maintained that, since Pedagogy does not constitute a theoretical body with an empirical basis, much less does it have a positivist character, this discipline constitutes a science, but rather a theory - practice, which deals with the 'ought to be' of education. education, for which he maintained that a 'science of education' of an explanatory nature still had to be founded, which dealt with the 'being' of education" (AV Martín. 2007, p. 28.)

- The third reason is contextual. First, the existence and influence of the social sciences in a greater state of epistemological maturity (sociology, Economics, etc.), which occupied a space that Pedagogy was not adequately addressing, was setting the tone for educational work. Second, if we accept that knowledge, including scientific knowledge, is a cultural construction influenced by the meaning that people give; and culture in education described only educational practice, then it is easy to understand that pedagogy was devalued as a science. Third, another element that converges in the meaning that was being given to Pedagogy at that historical moment was the little development of its epistemology. Why did the French, having greatly developed epistemology in recent times, maintain their vision of "educational sciences"? The reason detailed below could be an explanation.

- The fourth reason has a connotation of cultural tradition. One hundred or one hundred and fifty years of conceptual tradition is very difficult to dissolve. One hundred years of conditioning and inertia aimed at believing the same thing can lead to conviction and dogma. One hundred and fifty years of believing, quite rightly, that their explanations are the most satisfactory, can be translated into a shared approach that guides the rationality of a scientific community. This explains the difficulty in developing new rationalities, due to the fear of not being branded by the scientific community as "heterodox," "heretic," "traitor" or "irrational." Without wishing or intending it, in an unconscious act, the intellectual influenced by these dogmas directs his rationality (what Thomas Kuhn called, acting according to the canons of normal science).Juan Amós Comenio (1998, p. 32) declared it in 1657. "Just as the tongue strongly affected by one flavor cannot easily distinguish another, in the same way the understanding concerned in one sense does not sufficiently attend to what comes from another direction." This indicates that it is very human to behave according to your dogmas. That, yesterday, today and always, human beings will cling to their beliefs, and that this will make it difficult to understand other proposals.

You have to be a "revolutionary scientist" to break those pre-established paradigms or dogmas. The metaphor of how a paradigm is formed and the influence it has on man's behavior, which circulates on the Internet, is very graphic to understand this. "A scientist put 5 monkeys in a cage, and in the center a ladder and, on top of it, a basket with bananas. When a monkey came up, the scientist threw cold water on the others. After some time, when one monkey came up, the others attacked him for fear of the cold water. After some time, none of the monkeys dared to go up. Then, the scientist brought a new monkey that he made climb the ladder; being beaten by the others, the new member did not climb any further. A second monkey was substituted and the same thing happened. The first substitute enthusiastically participated in the beating. A third was changed, and the fact is repeated. When he replaced the last ones, there was a group of five monkeys who never received a cold water bath, and yet continued to hit the one who tried to get to the bananas. If it were possible to ask them why they hit him, the answer would be: I don't know, things have always been done that way here."

All these reasons try to explain why a community as lucid as the French one, until now, maintains the belief in the concept "the sciences of education." Fully analyzing the starting question of this item, which position has greater epistemological status? We begin by asking, currently, what is the epistemological status of the position "the sciences of education"?

1. Entering the epistemological terrain forces us to discriminate some aspects of a science. We will begin by analyzing the object of study. The first thing that must be clear is that education is not the object of study of sociology, economics or psychology, but of Pedagogy. The second thing is that given the complexity of life, certain sciences with their perspective and problems were applied to specific sectors of human activities. Just as Economics was applied to education, agriculture, mining, etc., the same as Psychology was applied to the labor, educational, etc. field.

Autonomous sciences, such as sociology, psychology, economics, etc., have their own object of study, and extend their principles, laws and theories to specific problems (from their perspective) or specific sectors of a given reality to extract new ones. Knowledge that would be applicable in that sector of reality. "Which is why some authors call it 'sciences applied to education' (R. Follari 1989), that is, autonomous sciences applied to a specific sector of human activity. These autonomous sciences generate an applicative discourse for that sector, but not an explanatory discourse like the scientific one (although the Association of American Psychologists does not consider it to be an Applied Psychology to education). In this way, the field of the so-called "educational sciences" would be recognized "as a scientific-technological field of application rather than as a field of basic research."(AV Martín 2007, p. 27).

Each autonomous science, from its perspective and problems, independently generates certain information about a sector of the educational reality. This parceled knowledge must serve the pedagogue, as his specific background, to develop the pedagogical discourse that recovers this knowledge to describe and explain the educational fact, from the educational perspective and problems. So it is not that Education has its sciences; Rather, it is the autonomous sciences that apply their knowledge to specific sectors of education. Quintana (1997, p. 67) explained it in the following way, "what unites them is the study of education (material object); What distinguishes them is the aspect they study (formal object). For education, in effect, is a double semantic reality, according to in infieri or in facto: the first is studied by Pedagogy, and the second by the educational sciences.

2. Another argument that is used to classify Pedagogy as part of the Educational Sciences is that it does not have an autonomous field of action, since that field of action, education, is shared with other autonomous sciences. Therefore, it is correct that it is only one of the many sciences that studies the same object of study. But, that argument is questionable, even ignoring the explanation given in the previous paragraphs.

When it is questioned that Pedagogy does not have its own field of action and that the field is dominated by psychology, sociology, anthropology, etc., it is not having understood that an object can be the subject of study of many autonomous sciences, for example, man. Man in his relationship with others is studied by sociology, man in his relationship with culture and his history is studied by anthropology, man in his relationship with his behavior and feelings is studied by psychology, etc., But, The same object of study cannot be studied by two different sciences from the same perspective, clearly illustrated by the previous examples. So Sociology studies or applies its principles to education from its special perspective; the same happens with Psychology, Economics, etc. Similarly, Pedagogy studies education with its special perspective, generating its knowledge that addresses educational facts to meet its own objectives.

Another question is when one science addresses the object of study of another with its approaches and objectives: in that case one could speak of scientific intrusion, or the development of a new science that would be generated on the borders of both. In the first case, "intrusive" science would be losing its identity. In the second case, it would be a productive act since a new science is developed, there are multiple cases: biophysics, biochemistry, physical chemistry, etc.

Experience shows that the marginal participation of different sciences in an object of study does not convert that portion of science into an autonomous science. Rather, it is part of his science, it becomes a class, a "species" of his science. For example, Economics, when it is aimed at studying agriculture, is called Agricultural Economics (A), when it is aimed at studying the company, it is called Microeconomics (B), when it studies education it is called Educational Economics (C). A, B, C are still economies, rather they are specificities of the Economy. So, we can classify Economy as: A, B and C. For that reason, in the name the noun "Economy" is put first and then the adjective "Agricultural". Basically, things are defined by the substantive (it is their nature) and not by their accidents (adjectives), adjectives help specify the noun. The noun exists without the adjective existing, the adjective has no meaning without the presence of the noun.

Therefore, it is inappropriate to consider the segment of science that participates in an object of study, as if they were an autonomous science of that object of study. You cannot change the adjective into a noun. Another example, Agronomy is the discipline that studies the production and health of plants, however, Economics participates to know the costs and profitability of crops (sector of the economy called Agricultural Economy), Statistics to know the percentages, averages, percentiles in production (sector of statistics called Agricultural Statistics), Chemistry participates with its fertilizers, chemical quality of soils (Agricultural Chemistry), Sociology studies agricultural and producer organizations (Rural Sociology) , etc., each of them is a class of its science, no one would make the mistake of saying that those are the Agronomic Sciences. Although it is admitted that these disciplines are useful for developing agronomic sciences, they do not constitute agronomic sciences. This same reasoning must be applied to Education, and accept that the support of other sciences demonstrates the complexity of the educational fact.

Therefore, educational sciences do not exist; rather, what

exists is the part of a science that is responsible for studying the application of that science in education.

3. Admit that Pedagogy is only a science that integrates other sciences, a kind of coordinator of sciences, without producing theories and laws, taking advantage of what other sciences do, In factis to consider Pedagogy a parasitic science, a science that is not science (according to the current name). That was the position of John Dewey (1968), when he says that Pedagogy is a discipline "without its own (theoretical) content" and that it only develops as a field of application of theories that come from different social sciences such as Sociology, Economics, etc. Claudia Pontón Ramos (2002) reaffirms what Dewey said in the following way:

John Dewey was not concerned that the Science of Education did not have its own content, as long as this content was provided by other social sciences, since according to his epistemological conception, science must inevitably have, to be such, a practical theoretical character. , placing emphasis on the scientific-applied nature of the discipline*(, p. 120)*.

Accepting this position is so serious that It would imply admitting that Pedagogy would not make sense as a branch of knowledge. Quintana (1997, p. 66) expresses it in the following way.

Pedagogical knowledge would be reduced to the principles set forth by the psychology of education, the economics of education, the history of education, the sociology of education and other educational sciences: apart from them, Pedagogy would have nothing to say. Pedagogy would be an empty name, a scientific illusion, a term, in short, that must disappear.

If this were so, we would understand why the French were repugnant to that term and its meaning. To admit this nature of

Pedagogy is to denigrate it; it is to accept that it is dispensable as a branch of knowledge to study educational facts.

But is that true? Absolutely not, if we don't do an exercise. Let's put all the sciences in a row, looking at education and keeping its objective in mind: to train people. Let's separate the Economy. Could we generate knowledge that allows us to describe and explain the formation of people without the Economy? The answer is yes. Let's continue with the exercise. Let's separate Sociology. Could we generate knowledge that allows us to describe and explain the formation of people without Sociology? The answer is yes. And without Psychology, would we achieve the same thing? For sure yes. Although it is admitted that there would be more difficulties with this, or that its explanations would not be as satisfactory, just as Physics would have problems without Mathematics. But there is no doubt that pedagogical theories and laws would continue to be produced, although at less speed and depth.

Let's do the exercise the other way around, let's remove Pedagogy. What information does economics give us about education? It gives us information about the cost of educating each student, the future income of a good student, etc. What information does sociology give us about education? Provides information about the teacher's role: whether he is a democrat or authoritarian, the social structure of the students in the classroom, etc. Is this information about the person's formation? Absolutely NO. Therefore, the other sciences are complementary, and Pedagogy is the vital or essential science for that objective.

4. All this leads us to admit that Pedagogy has its own epistemological status as an autonomous science. In this sense Touriñan (1987, p.268) stated:

When we talk about Pedagogy as a science of education, we want to affirm that, epistemologically - due to the way of knowing - and anthologically - due to the area of reality that is studied -, education is susceptible to autonomous scientific study. Pedagogy as a science of education is an autonomous scientific discipline like psychology, biology, sociology, etc.

And R. Nassif (1980, p. 53) adds:

Attributing the character of positive science to Pedagogy is nothing more than recognizing its capacity to obtain knowledge of a fact that corresponds to it as an object. To achieve this, you are allowed to use many procedures, including the universal ones of description, observation and experimentation.

In this direction the author completely agrees.

5. Until now, the technological nature that many educational theorists give to Pedagogy has not been discussed at all, because it will be the subject of the next chapter, since this work defends the idea that the technological aspect of education is not has Pedagogy but Didactics. Lorenzo García Areto (p. 45) stated:

Pedagogy must perform basic functions such as the control of external actions - as already indicated - and the prescription and offer of educational actions that must cover all human dimensions, use all types of cultural elements and be communicated by the most various educational agents through different procedures. [...] These are all arguments that drive us to demand a scientific-technological conception of Pedagogy. [...] These technological approaches to educational activities are essential because the rational proposal of objectives, the effectiveness in the development of the action, its temporality, as well as its economic profitability must be taken into account (Sarramona, 1986:135). The substantivity and identity of Pedagogy as educational science and technology is considered fundamental (Castillejo, 1987:18). [...] This scientific-technological conception referred to is being postulated in Spain by a good part of educational theorists.

Pedagogy as a science has its own division, its branches that are classified according to the criteria used. If the criterion of its approach is used, then its typology would be: General Pedagogy, Differential Pedagogy, and Special Pedagogy. If the criterion of the space or group to be addressed is used, then its typology would be: Labor Pedagogy, Adult Pedagogy, Family Pedagogy, Institutional and Social Pedagogy. If we use the content criterion: Experimental pedagogy, systemic pedagogy. And thus, according to the criteria used, Pedagogy could be classified.

2.3 THE NATURE OF PEDAGOGY

In accordance with everything established, the concept of Pedagogy that is proposed is the following: Pedagogy is a social science whose object of study is education, whose purpose is to describe, explain and understand educational facts. It is necessary to consider everything that involves the concept of EDUCA-TION (detailed in the previous chapter) to understand the scope of pedagogy. This definition incorporates an important epistemological component in the process of pedagogical research or when scientific research is carried out in education: the need to complement scientific knowledge and other subjective components to achieve the explanation and understanding of the educational fact. This implies encompassing more than one research paradigm when researching in education.

THE NATURE OF DIDACTIC

Didactics is a discipline that has generated great controversies, it has been elevated by many schools in Europe and Latin America to the rank of science, however, there are some positions that deny it that character, rather placing it on the level of technology. Can it be demonstrated that didactics is science? Can it be demonstrated that didactics is technology? The next chapter is dedicated to this.

CHAPTER 3

THE NATURE OF DIDACTIC

The wise man can change his mind. The fool, never.

— IMMANUEL KANT

The most difficult thing to learn in life is which bridge to cross and which bridge to burn.

— BERTRAND RUSSELL

JA Comenio. (1998, p. 78) in his greatest work Didactica Magna, chapter XX, item 23, he wrote (bold letters were used to highlight the message):

Explain the differences of things well to obtain a clear and evident knowledge of all of them. That well-known saying contains much: He who knows how to make distinctions will teach well. The multitude of things overwhelms the learner and the variety leads to confusion if the remedy is not applied; for the first, the order so that they are undertaken one after the other, and for the second, the careful observation of the differences so that it appears clearly how some things differ from others. Only this provides clear and certain evident knowledge, because the truth and variety of things lie in their differences.

This reflection by Comenius encourages the elaboration of this subchapter, making an effort to orderly differentiate the concepts, categories, etc., since as will be seen later there are a multitude of them, and thus properly establish the nature of Didactics. We hope this claim is fulfilled.

3.1 AVATARS IN THE CONCEPTION OF DIDACTIC.

To begin, let us comment on what Félix E. González Jiménez (1990) pointed out:

Many defining approaches have been made about Didactics, almost all of them analogical: it is like one of those important things that Saint Augustine said that we all know what they are, unless they ask us. But this does not justify this as a substitution that seems to be intended with the use of other less clear and less practical terms and concepts. It was said that Didactics was an art, then that it could be considered a science, then as science and at the same time technology, later almost exclusively as technology; now it tends to be silenced" (p. 34)

This is what happens with Didactics, when we ask: What is Didactics and what are the foundations? Generally we find a gap in the answers given. Didactics as a field of knowledge has undergone many transformations due to the action of some scholars who typified it according to their pretensions, or due to the evolution of the discipline itself.A. Adúriz-Bravo and M. Izquierdo Aymerich (2002, pp. 131-134),They propose five stages that describe the evolution of Didactics:

1. *Adisciplinary stage.* *From the end of the 19th century to the mid-1950s, productions in the field that we today call Science Didactics are scarce and heterogeneous. The disparity of these productions and the lack of connection between their authors do not allow us to assume the existence of Science Didactics. [...]*

2. *Technological stage.* *This stage began in the '50s and '60s. [...]. The efficiency-oriented science teaching of this stage aims to rely on the scientific knowledge generated in external disciplinary areas; generates a base of recommendations, resources and methodological techniques. [...]It is because of its willingness to intervene in the classroom without dealing with the development of basic knowledge, that we can characterize it as technological. It is interesting to note that this technological conception of Didactics still remains rooted in many countries, particularly in those where scientifically based Didactic research is not yet very developed. [...]*

3. *Protodisciplinary stage.* *In the mid-1970s, consensus grew about the existence of a new field of studies; researchers in science teaching began to consider themselves members of the same community [...] The research problems of teaching will initially be linked to the learning of specific science content; [...]. This is why we can speak of a protodisciplinary stage, in which several schools that are not sufficiently structured compete to establish themselves as the theoretical basis of the community. [...]*

4. Emerging discipline. *In the '80s, science educators in leading countries began to worry about the theoretical coherence of the body of accumulated knowledge. [...]. The conceptual self-revision that thus begins, characterized by interdisciplinary openness (Astolfi and Develay, 1989), leads at the end of the decade to the consensus that constructivism, in its Didactic version, is the common theoretical basis for the majority. part of the field studies [...].*

5. Consolidated discipline. *During recent years, despite the scarcity of studies on the discipline (parallel to the explosion in the number of studies in the discipline), there is a more or less generalized opinion about the growing consolidation of science didactics as a body theoretically and as an academic community (Gil-Pérez et al., 2000). [...]. Teachability is then seen as a central argument to sustain the disciplinarity of Didactics, since its necessary condition is the existence of a structure of its own coherence, transposable and disseminated.*

This division of the stages in the development of Didactics is a theoretical effort that is worth consolidating. However, the criteria used to establish the division correspond more to the way a scientific or technological discipline is defined, and not so much to the substance itself. The criteria used are basically two: the formation of a community, and the amount of studies or research carried out in the discipline. They are criteria linked more to appearance than to the essence itself. So the classification itself is called into question, and if that were the tendency to characterize a discipline we should be concerned. In the chapter where the nature of Pedagogy was described, this issue was warned (remember the characteristics that a discipline must meet for it to become scientific).

How much do phenomenal criteria influence the characterization of a discipline? In our opinion, very little. In reality, they are complementary and not substantive criteria; when this happens, the constructed building is easily destroyed. Miguel A. Zabalza Beraza (2007) pointed it out as follows:

> *Ruling, giving an opinion or imparting doctrine is not the same as presenting proven facts. Didactic knowledge (as a space of human activity where knowledge is constructed and applied) will be all the more scientific the closer it approaches and respects the conditions of rationality, systematicity and justification of its principles. Processes and products. (p. 497)*

Given these words, what matters is that when presenting knowledge, it must be done with the greatest rigor and foundation possible. In reality, there are few works where this logical and epistemological rigor is perceived to determine the nature of Didactics. Very few works have analyzed the essential requirements to define the nature of a discipline, as a type of knowledge, the structure of the theories that are part of the disciplinary content, etc. Rather, the analysis of marginal criteria, quantitative reports of the appearance of the discipline, is observed in many works as dominant foundations to establish the characteristic of Didactics. Some statements from Didactics scholars are also read that state the characteristics, without detailing the foundations of their proposals, this generates a void in the study. Then there are other works that with astonishing intrepidity launch postulations of the nature of Didactics without proper support. Furthermore, there are investigations that only mechanically transcribe proposals from other authors, without considering the context and historical time in which it was written.

Another interesting topic is the one raised by FE González Jiménez and M. Díez Barrabés (2004), in the summary of their work, they pointed out, "Specific didactics are a significant part of general didactics, forms of its concretion." (p. 253). It is noted that the General Didactics contain the Specific Didactics, therefore, it is established that epistemologically the nature of both is similar, and there is no discussion about that. In agreement with this conclusion of F. Gonzales and M. Díez, for the purposes of the epistemological analysis, it is indistinct whether to describe the General Didactics or the Specific Didactics, therefore, in the work the general definitions on the nature of both.

In this global moment of great accessibility to information, it is perceived in the cloud of virtual and physical information that the meaning of Didactics is very varied. There is a great ambiguity or polysemy of the term, which generates confusion and ambiguity. When analyzing why this multiplicity of meanings exist, the following underlying or explicit reasons were found:

a. When concepts provided in different historical spaces and times are compared and discrimination is not made. F. Larroyo (1963, p. 218) puts it as follows:

> *Some authors give the term "Didactics" a too broad meaning: they include within it all the problems concerning the science of education. Historically, it had such vast meaning in the 18th century, when Comenius vulgarized the term, calling his most important pedagogical work the Great Didactic.*

> *As for the philological root of the word, we already said that teaching, instructing, is said in Greek didascoo. [...]. The first to use the name didactic to call the researcher who studies the principles and rules of teaching was Ratke. This is confirmed by the document written in 1613 by some German teachers under the title "Appreciation of Didactics or the Art of Teaching", by Ratke.*

Which of these conceptions of Didactics is current? Which has a greater logical, epistemological or empirical foundation? In this case, the conception of Didactics goes from one extreme pole to the other. For Comenio, Didactics is related to all the problems of Education, a kind of super discipline. However, for Ratke Didactics is limited solely and exclusively to the way of teaching.

Modern authors such as Daniel Feldman (2010) are closer to Ratke, emphasizing teaching as the field of action of Didactics, but clarifying that this field is more complex:

> *Teaching is not just about teaching a group of people, but about teaching in large organizations to a huge number of people. The concerns in which Didactics works are those of a professional who works in a large organization subject to restrictions that include working conditions, the program, the agreement with other teachers, the framework of coexistence that is accepted, or any type of conditioning factor that frames the teaching task. (p. 10)*

The same was indicated by A. de Camilloni, MC Davini, et al (1995, p.27) "Didactics is the theory of teaching inherited and indebted to other disciplines that, when dealing with teaching, constitutes itself as an offerer and giver of theory in the field of social action and knowledge.

Based on the previous evidence (which is part of a set of evidence), it is shown how a conceptualization loses validity, loses its theoretical force by not being considered valid, by not being cited by colleagues from the same community, while others they consolidate. From here we draw a conclusion, readers should consider Comenius' contribution as part of his culture, and Ratke to develop his discipline. Or otherwise, conclude that Comenius is right, but it is a duty to substantiate the conclusion as rigorously as possible.

b. When they maintain different origins in their conceptualization.

First, F. Best (1988, p. 165) points out the origin of Didactics from Pedagogy: "Didactics replace, with a much more marked scientific character, the "Special Pedagogies" of yesteryear. [...] But it is undeniable that Pedagogy emerges, once again, from one of its components, which is practical knowledge." This explanation, to a certain extent, invites us to think that Didactics is a part of Pedagogy, a branch of it, a discipline that is partly theoretical (due to the scientific nature of Pedagogy) and partly practical (due to the field of action itself). of Didactics).

Second, by indicating that Didactics constitutes a discipline that goes beyond its strictly technical (non-technological) nature and that has edges of science, N. Abbagnano, and A. Visalberghi, (1992, p. 416) describe that:

> *Lombardo-Radice [...]. He had a concrete historical vision of the Didactic activity that led him to restore to it a large part of the credit that Gentile had almost completely taken away from it; However, Didactics cannot be limited to being a repertoire of rules, nor pretend that it is derived abstractly from scientific or pseudo-scientific systems, but must be carried out as a perennial renewal, as a perennial invention, on a historically given and scientifically organized basis.*

And finally, when Didactics is another version of Pedagogy. C. Álvarez de Zayas (2004, p. 142) pointed out "Didactics is a systemic, efficient Pedagogy; That is to say, in Didactics the laws are expressed more obviously."

Due to its origin, Didactics is more of a technical discipline (Gentile), but it evolved and became a practical discipline with theoretical connotations (F. Best's position) and then became a science itself (Álvarez de Zayas's position). These assessments are reasonable, Didactics goes beyond being a simple technique. The problem is what follows: What does it mean to be a theoretical-practical science? Is it really being science? Or does it mean that it is applied science? Or does it constitute technology? The conclusion that can be obtained is that the lack of precision in the use of terms is harmful for the company to base a proposal. This lack of precision leads to confusion among those initiated in the field.

*c. When a serious and well-founded study on the nature of Didactics has not been carried out, that is, when the logical and epistemological analysis is very poor.*The context that explains this situation occurs at the time when Didactics, whether General or

Specific, were incorporated into the Educational Sciences (Pedagogy, Educational Psychology, etc.), difficulties began to find the corresponding foundation. . This was aggravated when, on the one hand, the desire to scientificize the discipline advanced (when "being" science was to be on the Olympus of knowledge) and on the other hand, the epistemological terminology was clarified and the concepts of basic science began to be differentiated, applied science, technology, etc., at which time the theorists played with expressions, which they could hardly support.

H. Dámaris Díaz (1999, p. 110) highlights these indefinitions by indicating: "It is worth remembering that Didactics is a discipline that has experienced, like the other Social Sciences, the vicissitudes of epistemological, conceptual and methodological indefinitions. In principle, because some authors have not achieved their delimitation as a field of knowledge, and other authors have made their objectives fit with those of Pedagogy."

An exemplary case of these epistemological and conceptual vicissitudes would be in the work of A. Medina Rivilla (2007) who states (they are put in bold to highlight messages that illustrate what is to be demonstrated):

Didactics has developed the technological perspective from scientific rationality, [...], given that it is a science [...]. The technological perspective is based on the conception of the instructional-training process as a reality susceptible to systematization and scientific-innovative development.

Didactic knowledge is generated, in this perspective, as rigorous, planned knowledge and doing, carried out with efficiency and effectiveness and valued for its coherence and adjustment to the scientific framework and the intended teleology.

Didactic technology *has contributed to the conception and training practice the terms of systematization, optimization, effectiveness, efficiency, quality, control, regulation, feedback, etc.,* *aiming for the permanent improvement of the practice and the use of resources, generalizing the most positive aspects of the know and do, for the benefit of each human being and society as a whole. (p. 432)*

***Didactics has technological approaches among its approaches**, which prescribes the training action, supported by scientific knowledge. (p.435)*

The author of the previous quote shows us three very useful lessons for work purposes. We are in perfect agreement with lessons two and three, but the first shows a certain insolvency. These are:

- Not all theorists in a discipline clearly differentiate the nature of science from the nature of technology. The author affirms that Didactics is a science, but then points out that the knowledge generated is technological knowledge. There is an apparent contradiction if each sentence were taken literally, since science generates scientific knowledge. Or it could be considered a confusion if the author defined said science as applied science, and established that applied science is equal to technology.
- Didactic knowledge is prescriptive, regulative, normative, whose aim is to improve, to take advantage of resources to benefit the individual and society (we agree on this).
- The criteria used to assess didactic knowledge are efficiency, effectiveness, optimization, etc. (we agree on that).

These last two lessons will be vital to establish the difference between scientific and technological knowledge, which will be analyzed in detail later.

Another example is seen in the work of ML Eder and A. Adúriz Bravo (2001) "Epistemological approach to the relationships between the Didactics of Natural Sciences and General Didactics," where they make an interesting review of the virtues and limitations of the currents. Epistemological, but they put as an epistemological foundation to establish the scientific nature of Didactics only a quote from R. Porlán from 1992 ("The Didactics of Sciences"), but very little or almost nothing is offered regarding the internal analysis of Didactics. The quote from R. Porlán (1992) is:

> *Science Didactics has undergone an important clarification process. It has gone from being a set of technological curricular prescriptions, which sought to transfer a positivist logic of science and its method to the school, without taking into account, for this purpose, a set of mediating variables that exist in teaching systems. -learning, to be a possible discipline (...), of a practical and complex nature, which already has, although rudimentary, some of the essential requirements to be considered as such (...) a clearer epistemological location, an incipient community, means of communication and contrast (magazines and conferences, etc.), a body of specific knowledge, as well as an object of study and a problem recognized by said community (pp. 68-71).*

This quote with the same words was repeated by R. Porlán (1998, p. 178)

The conclusion obtained is that an investigation or study cannot support its most important and transcendental proposal, only with gratuitous statements or with uncontrasted statements.

d. When a category developed by other theorists is used differently or incorrectly, without proper foundation. An example of these impertinent uses that lead to a series of digressions regarding the nature of Didactics, is the work of Javier Suso López, and M. Eugenia Fernández Fraile (2001) when they wrote (the categories are highlighted in bold to make them stand out):

We thus defend a conception of Didactics as an autonomous science, which maintains relationships of contiguity and complementarity, not only with Linguistics and Applied Linguistics, but also with Educational Sciences. (p. 21). Or when they point out that:

"Didactics is not a mere technical adaptation of prior linguistic knowledge. Didactics constitutes a 'Theory of application,' a 'Technology'; That is, it has an inherent reflective component about its object, which it will establish from the apprehensions and descriptions of linguistic science, like the rest of the applied sciences with respect to the corresponding basic science" (p. 22).

With this example one wonders: Is Didacta autonomous science, applied science or technology? What did the authors of the book mean? If it is an autonomous science, it implies that it has an object of study different from all other disciplines, including Pedagogy. Is that true? To know if it is applied science or technology, in the previous chapter the differences between basic science, applied and technology, so it would be pointless to repeat these concepts.

On the other hand, it is not strange that at the level of the university community, teachers and students of Higher Education are confused about the use and management of these concepts, JA Acevedo Díaz., Á. Vázquez Alonso, Mª A. Manassero Mas and P. Acevedo Romero (2003, pp. 365, 367) showed a table (partly reproduced below) showing "the percentages that correspond to the results of the evaluations made on large samples of students and teachers in Mallorca using the Questionnaire of Opinions and Beliefs about Science, Technology and Society –COCTS".

Table 1.-Examples of beliefs of students and teachers about the meaning of technology and its relationships with science

Core beliefs	Students (%)	Future teachers (%)	Active teachers (%)
(10211) Technology is applied science	20.9	37.0	45.7

With these figures, extrapolating (if possible) to all of Spain or the Hispanic world, it is not surprising that the community of pedagogues or didacts do not know how to differentiate whether Didactics is applied science, or technology or autonomous science. For this to happen, it is likely that there are a multitude of causes, but there is no doubt that a very influential one is in the training of pedagogues or didacts. J. Acevedo Díaz (1998) puts it this way:

The vast majority of attempts made to introduce some knowledge of technology in science teaching, from the perspective of integrated science with technology, have contributed [...] to favor its erroneous identification with applied science. This image, deeply rooted popularly, has been spreading from science through scientific dissemination, science teaching and the Didactics of experimental sciences itself.

Another example of inaccurate use of terms is seen in the excellent doctoral thesis of A. Adúriz Bravo (2001), when he develops a proposal to demonstrate the scientific nature of Didactics (especially the sciences). To do this, he uses some categories that, in our opinion, are used inappropriately, leading him to err in his conclusions. Some examples (the categories will be highlighted in bold to highlight them) are the following:

"The thesis we support here is that Science Didactics, as it is a scientific discipline, can be modeled with the same theoretical tools that serve any scientific discipline."(p. 289)

He also points out, "The conception of science that we present here, and which is compatible with realism, [...]. Science, then, is seen as a way of representing the world capable of actively intervening in it" (p. 295).

Then he writes "In particular, we can characterize Science Didactics, within a model of hypothetical rationality, as a science of design [...]. When we talk about Science Didactics as techno-science" (p. 297)

First, he points out that Realism supports his conception of science (that science is theory and also transforms reality). The truth is that neither the naïve realism (of the scholastic philosophers), nor the scientific realism of Popper or Bunge (as previously reviewed, Bunge makes a clear distinction on this matter), nor the constructive realism of Giere, or the scientific realism Critics of Niiniluoto promote science to intervene directly in the world, but maintain the position that the most important goal of science is the search for truth, or providing satisfactory explanations. By forcing things, an indirect intervention of science in the world could be indicated, it could be through its predictive nature. Why is this situation criticized? Because it can be interpreted that this proposal has support from authorities in the matter, when the reality is not. Furthermore, the opinion of the authorities should not even matter, the use of empirical or rational evidence should matter more.

Regarding the term "the Science of design" (a priori accepting its existence and differentiating it from Technology) it generates a gnoseological problem. As a premise, we start from the fact that Didactics, being considered a scientific discipline, must be located within the social sciences (if you want to force things, you can place them in the natural sciences, and if we push a little, in the spiritual sciences).). However, Didactics is said to belong to or be a Science of Design. This situation generates blatant contradictions.

- First, because any Design Science, accepting that it exists, does not belong to the field of natural, social or spiritual sciences, but to the field of Artificial Sciences.

- Second, the dominant rationalities are different between the natural or social sciences and the artificial sciences. Rationality in Design Sciences according to WJ Gonzales (2007, pp. 4-6) is adaptive, very limited (both by its reasoning processes and by the search for results) and evaluative (aimed at solving problems of objectives, processes and results); while the natural and social sciences have a formal-logical, cognitive, normative, epistemic and intentional rationality.

- Third, the purposes of the natural or social or spiritual sciences are totally different from the purposes of the design sciences. Until now, Design Sciences use the "scientification" of previous processes to achieve concrete, tangible goals that transform a reality (they are very close to Technology), different from the natural or social sciences that scientifically study the facts (processes) to know them, or explain them.

Regarding the Technology category. In figure 10.2 and its explanation (p.296) of the aforementioned doctoral thesis, technoscience is presented as a link between science and technology. This assertion is contradictory with the definitions that he selected and put on the previous page (p. 295), but, more seriously, it contradicts B. Latour (1992), who introduced the term to the scientific community. For Latour, "technoscience" is a set that contains science and technology. It is not a mediator, it is the set that expresses the continuum of scientific work, which describes the strong interaction of science and technology.

Beyond Adúriz's internal contradictions, and the differences in understanding with B. Latour, creator of the term, the use of the term "technoscience" makes it difficult to adequately distinguish the difference between what is applied and technical science.

For this reason, M. Bunge (2002,p. 6)In his prologue, he challenged intellectuals to:

1. Defend basic research from pragmatist and neoliberal attacks. Highlight that new scientific knowledge, although it does not have immediate practical applications, enriches culture as much as art and the humanities enrich it. This task of defending disinterested research against the philistines requires, at a minimum, a clear distinction between basic, applied and technical science, as well as an evaluation of their respective functions in modern society. Unfortunately, fashionable sociologism-constructivism-relativism denies this distinction by speaking of "technoscience" and affirming that everything is a social construction or convention. Therefore, far from making positive contributions to scientific-technical policy, it inspires a utilitarian policy that requires that the so-called "technoscience" only produce results of immediate practical use.

B. Latour was tasked with analyzing science in action: studying what scientists did in laboratories and the development of engineers' prototypes. What he observed inspired him to develop the concept of "technoscience": he perceived a strong interaction, so he felt stimulated to create the neologism. He is sure that he also felt protected by what was happening in the frontier scientific disciplines, which by forming fields of action of the intercepted sciences, such as biochemistry, or physical-chemistry, etc., created new sciences. However, theory must be differentiated from meta-theory, and the task of the discipline with the classification of the knowledge generated by that discipline. If the logic of "technoscience" were extrapolated, and were brought to the relationship between philosophy and science, as, for example, WO Quine (1974) mentioned in his book "Natural Genres," "I see philosophy not as an a priori propaedeutic or fundamental work for science, but as a continuum with science. I see philosophy and science as crew members of the same ship", so we would say that in the face of that great interaction, for example, Physics would be "Philociencia" or Cienciafilo," nothing more ridiculous. The strong interaction between one discipline and another, and even the use of cognitive domains from another discipline, does not modify its nature.

If we also remember that the expression "technoscience" for Bunge is barbaric, and for Niinilouto a weak and unproductive expression (reviews presented in the previous chapter), the only thing that confirms is that many times theorists do not use words appropriately.

Another example of the inappropriate use of terms is observed in the work of R. Porlán Ariza (1992) in the quote reviewed above (part of it is transcribed), where expressions are used incorrectly:

*Science Didactics has undergone an important clarification process. It has gone from being a set of technological curricular prescriptions, which sought to transfer a positivist logic of science and its method to the school, without taking into account, for this purpose, a set of mediating variables that exist in teaching systems. -learning, to be a possible discipline." (*Quote repeated by Porlán in 1998, p. 178)

Porlán is using the category "possible discipline" to refer to the nature of Didactics. This is a category introduced by S. Toulmin (1972). Porlán (1998, p. 175) described and used Toulmin's classification, so that category was not strange to him. But what is a possible discipline? A discipline is possible when said discipline can bring together or fulfill all the characteristics that a science must have (problematic, methodical, assumptions, community, etc.). Therefore, Porlán is telling us that Didactics has the potential to be a scientific discipline, which can meet the characteristics to be scientific, but he does not tell us that it is a scientific discipline. He does not say that Didactics meets the characteristics to be scientific. Then, 6 years later, Porlán (1998, p. 176) declares that "Didactics is an emerging discipline (it meets some of the requirements set forth), possible (its evolution indicates that it can meet all of them) and practical (its problems). Specific refer to scientific education).

As we see in the quote, Porlán affirms that Didactics is an "emerging and possible discipline." Porlán's emergent discipline category is similar to the meaning of Toulmin's diffuse discipline category, which is his theoretical reference. We make this simile, in order to compare the emergent discipline category with the possible discipline category. The emerging discipline (from Porlán, read the quote above) or diffuse discipline (from Toulmin (1972), read his classification) refer to disciplines that meet some of the requirements of a mature scientific discipline. Therefore, we can conclude that "emergent discipline" is the same as "diffuse discipline." Up to that point there is nothing strange, the problem is when he points out that Didactics is also a possible discipline. So, what Porlán tells us is the following: Didactics is an emerging or diffuse discipline, but also a possible discipline. Let's use logic to understand this:

A = Emerging discipline or diffuse discipline (discipline that meets some requirements to be scientific)

B = Possible discipline (discipline that is not compliant, but could be compliant in the future).

B is not A

Say that Didactics (D) is = A (emerging discipline) and B (possible discipline),

It is equal, D= (A, B),...... and if B = it is not A

It is accepting that D = A but it is also not A. Complete absurdity.

In many cases, theorists repeat a general assessment from a respected researcher, and the assessment is simply accepted as truth. Others, by not adequately reviewing the terminology, repeat the phrase, worse yet, they contaminate it with their desire or feelings, and affirm a truth that has not yet been proven.

Another example of incorrect use of the terms is found in A. Adúriz Bravo (1999/2000. p. 68) when maintaining that Didactics is an autonomous scientific discipline, he wrote, "From the theoretical point of view, we have modeled the disciplinarity and autonomy of Science Didactics (Adúriz-Bravo, in press) with the method of epistemic matrices (Samaja, 1994)".

Adúriz uses an expression that J. Samaja in his book Epistemology and Methodology (1999, p.140). He says regarding epistemic matrices:

[...] the concept of "conception of the world" conceiving it as a "general scheme" that is used by the common man in his daily life, as well as by the poet, the religious, the philosopher or the scientist.

I am going to propose calling this "conception of the world" an "epistemic matrix," to the extent that it operates in scientific work as a selection criterion for pre-existing metaphors or analogies in the leading experience of a given culture.

J Samaja throughout his book does not refer to epistemic matrices as "method" but as "conception of the world." The simile of epistemic matrices is that of paradigm, or disciplinary matrices (proposed by T. Kuhn), with the express consideration of how "a" way of thinking affects the activity you carry out. But, what it develops and operationalizes is the data matrix and data matrix systems. The data matrix in the research process is specified in the variable operationalization matrix.

The conclusion of this section, according to Confucius, is that the "confusion of concepts generates the problems of the world". In this case, the confusion in the understanding of the concepts generates a distortion of the proposals.

What a tangle of qualifiers for Didactics, we really ask ourselves: What is Didactics? Given the lack of unanimity or consensus among Didactic theorists regarding its nature, each indicated statement will be analyzed.

To answer all questions about the nature of Didactics, the philosophical system of science based on Popper's critical rationalism or scientific realism such as that of Bunge or Toulmin will be used. It is from this perspective that what is science or not is established. If some criticized the use of that system, what other philosophical system of science would you advise using? Of course each existing worldview has its own system of grading knowledge and its own concepts of what science is. If I used system A, I would be criticized by the followers of system B or by C. If I used B I would be criticized by A and by C. This system was selected because it is the best constructed and accepted in the community of scientists and epistemologists in the world. (If the thesis was dedicated exclusively to this topic, it would be obliged to carry out the analyzes according to each existing worldview). Going to the other extreme, not having a reference system would be very dangerous, not setting measurement parameters would be complicated to evaluate any discipline. Going ridiculous, without valid and reliable parameters, it could happen that according to my conception of the world or my personal epistemic matrix, any nonsense I say or do could be considered science.

3.2 IS DIDACTIC AN AUTONOMOUS SCIENCE?

There are many theorists who maintain that Didactics is an autonomous science. A. Adúriz-Bravo and M. Izquierdo Aymerich (2002, p. 136) are promoters of this idea, and they express it like this:

> *Our vision of Science Didactics is then that of a discipline that is currently autonomous, focused on the contents of science from the point of view of its teaching and learning (that is, a discipline with a largely epistemological basis), and nourished by the findings of other disciplines concerned with cognition and learning (psychology and those in the area of cognitive science [...]. Since its origins, Science Didactics has supported its autonomy in a systematic and scientific approach to education in science.*

Along the same lines, J. Suso López and Mª E. Fernández Fraile (2001, p. 21) stated "We thus defend a conception of Didactics as an autonomous science, which maintains relationships of contiguity and complementarity, not only with Linguistics. And Applied Linguistics, but also with Educational Sciences."

What criteria do theorists use to establish the scientificity and autonomy of Didactics, in this case specifics?

According to the work of A. Adúriz-Bravo and M. Izquierdo Aymerich (2002, p. 134), the criteria are the following:

The empirical indicators that support the maturity of Didactics are:

1. *The number of annual productions, which has grown exponentially (Gil-Pérez, 1996);*
2. *The consolidation of networks for the dissemination of results worldwide, such as important conferences in different subspecialties (Sanmartí, 1995);*
3. *The recognition of Science Didactics as a specific area of knowledge and as a postgraduate degree (Gil-Pérez et al., 2000); and*

    4. *The complexity and heuristic power of several of the didactic models formulated. These are beginning to have a structure widely recognized as scientific, and are becoming increasingly unified into general theoretical families.*

Then, D. Gil Pérez, J. Carrascosa Alís, and. F. Martínez Terrades (1999) propose the autonomy and scientific nature of Didactics in the following way:

Our hypothesis in this regard has been that Science Didactics was, in fact, being formed as a specific domain of knowledge, with the elements of a scientific discipline, such as: a scientific community, organs of expression, lines of defined research and, above all, an evolution towards generalized consensus and towards the integration of different aspects into coherent bodies of knowledge, with relevant contributions for work in the classroom and the training of science teachers. (p. 22)

In a previous recapitulation work (Gil, 1994) we referred to some first indicators that seemed to support our hypothesis. And in a recent doctoral thesis (Martínez-Terrades, 1998) we have delved into this study with results that reinforce the thesis of the emergence of Science Didactics as a scientific discipline. We will comment, as an example, on some of these results.

We will refer, first of all, to the evolution of the organs of expression and the number of published works. We find that the journal Science Education appeared in 1916, and we have to wait until 1963 for the Journal of Research in Science Teaching to appear and 1972 for the publication of Studies in Science. On the contrary, from the 1980s onwards numerous journals began to appear such as the European Journal of Science Education, Enseñanza de las Ciencias, The Austra Uan Journal of Science Education, ÁSTER, Science and Technological Education, the

Revista de Enseñanza de la Physics, O Ensino de Physics, Research in School, Didaskalia, Alambique, etc., etc., leading to the appearance of magazines specialized in specific aspects such as Science & Education (appeared in 1991), dedicated to the study of the role of history and philosophy of science in science teaching or Aliage, published since 1989 and focused on culture-science-technology interactions. In addition to this growth in the number of magazines, there has been a notable increase in their periodicity or the number of their pages. Thus, the International Journal of Science Education, which appeared in 1979 as the European Journal of Science Education, with four issues per year, currently publishes ten issues. And in Science Education, to cite another example, since its appearance until today the number of pages in each issue has practically tripled. (p. 23)

As can be seen in the arguments of the cited theorists, the foundations for giving scientificity and autonomy to Didactics are very quantitative, phenomenal, in appearance. Not to mention that the foundation is very poor, since it does not address what is essential. A deep analysis or characterization of didactic knowledge has been necessary to be able to differentiate that knowledge from other types, that is, there is valid information in each research work and in the investigations (since the seriousness of the investigations and publications will not be discussed).), but for example, if a publication exclusively referred to indicating methods or techniques or teaching materials to make the process more efficient, then the content would be purely technological. It is necessary to establish whether the body of knowledge contains its own laws and theories, and not, for example, is full of meta-theoretical works. The essential analysis would require identifying the configuration or structure of the didactic theory to differentiate it from other types of theories. So inventorying the number of magazines, published works, or members of a community, number of graduates, etc., are indicators that show a level of popularity or social acceptance, but do not guarantee the scientificity or autonomy of a discipline, because What is analyzed is the packaging and not the content.

What does it mean to be an autonomous science? An autonomous scienceIt is one that complies with the decatuple proposed by Bunge, or with the requirements proposed by Toulmin (remember what was detailed in the previous chapter on this matter). Therefore, it must have its own object of study that generates a problem, to be studied not only through the scientific method but also with its specific methods, based on its philosophical assumptions that guide the activity, to generate concepts, categories, laws. And theories that describe, explain/understand the facts studied, which will be accepted by a scientific community.

An autonomous science is independent of other sciences, but is not isolated from them. An autonomous science is an open system. It receives inputs from other sciences and technologies, but processes these and other inputs based on its purposes and structure, independent of other disciplines, to obtain a product that is specific to its nature. If Didactics were an autonomous science and independent of Pedagogy (and other sciences), a way to graph using the Euler/Venn diagram (figure No. 2) would be as follows.

Figure № 2 Independent, autonomous sets.

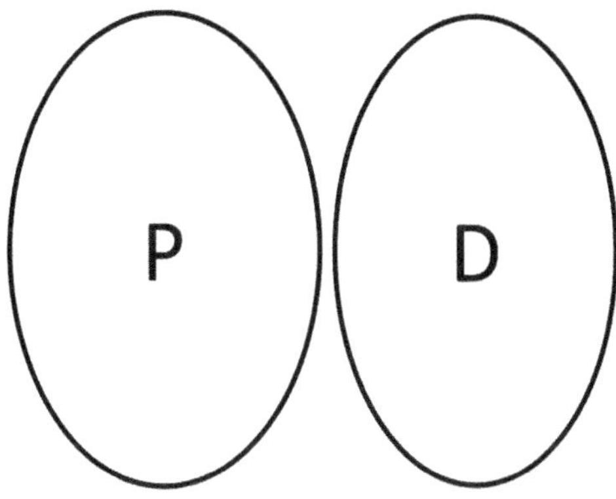

The interpretation of figure No. 2 would be the following: the existence of two sets, read the pedagogical science "P" and the science of Didactics "D," are completely independent, but with interaction between them. There are no common elements between these sets. It is similar to Mathematics which interacts with Biology, but they do not have common elements: their objects of study are different, their laws are different, etc. With the concepts and the quick message in Figure No. 2, the autonomous nature of Didactics will be analyzed.

In principle, in the hypothetical case that Pedagogy and Didactics are independent and autonomous sciences, they would be represented in figure No. 2. What does the empirical evidence say about it? At the purely experiential level, this vision is incompatible with reality itself, since in educational practice they use similar elements and there is a very strong cognitive and operational interaction, of a theory-empirical relationship (universal propositions versus facts), so that this autonomous conception of the two sciences is completely and automatically discarded.

Another way of expressing the relationship between two autonomous sciences with a certain interconnection can be graphed according to figure №3.

Figure № 3 Autonomous Sciences with common elements.

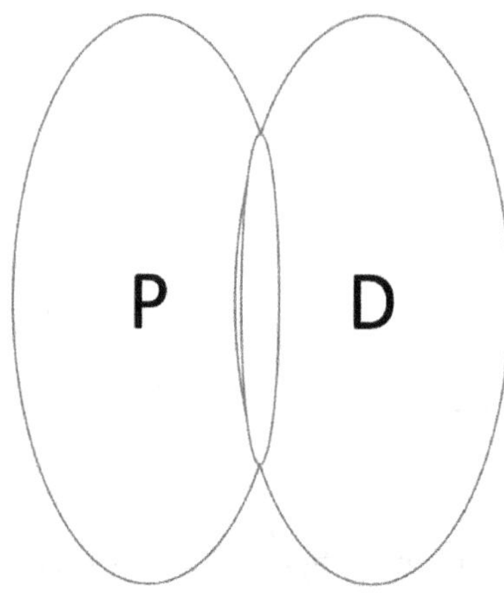

Q is the set that represents pedagogy and D is the set that represents Didactics. Both have common elements, but, to be considered autonomous sciences, substantively the elements have to be different.

Let's analyze the elements of sets. First the object of study. This must be specific to science, that is, autonomously studied by that science. An object cannot be studied by two different sciences from the same perspective. What is the object of the study of Didactics? Some theorists point out that the object of study of Didactics is the teaching process, others that it is the educational teaching process, and many others that it is the teaching-learning process. Now, is the teaching-learning process or educational teaching process or just the teaching process part of the educational process in general? We must agree that these processes are part of the general educational process, or Education. Teaching and learning form (or deform) the person or the professional, and this is properly educational. In conclusion, teaching-learning is an educational fact.

And, since Education with all its processes is studied by Pedagogy, it comes as a logical consequence that the teaching-learning process (it was selected because it is the most complex) is studied by Pedagogy. And with what perspective? Answer: with the educational perspective, that of forming a person. Conclusion: the teaching-learning process or teaching-educational process is an object of study of Pedagogy.

To accept that the educational teaching process or teaching-learning process or just the teaching process is an exclusively didactic and non-pedagogical fact, that is, independent of Pedagogy, it should be demonstrated that there is a difference with the educational teaching process or teaching-learning process studied. For Pedagogy. And if it were the same, then it should be demonstrated that he is studying it from a different perspective than educational, because the educational point of view is that of Pedagogy. There are no satisfactory answers to these concerns. There are only satisfactory answers when it is accepted that the teaching-learning, teaching-educational processes, or simply teaching, as educational facts are studied by Pedagogy with a formative perspective from the level of science, and are also studied by Didactics. , with the training perspective from the technological level.

Secondly, let's ask about the community of scientists. Is there a community of theorists who only do pedagogical research and other theorists who do didactic research? The blunt answer is no. The community of educational theorists carry out pedagogical research and can also carry out didactic research, not only in different research, but even in the same research.

Third, are the philosophical assumptions or values different when conducting research in these disciplines? Within a community of scientists, the substantive values and philosophical assumptions are similar. Therefore, in this element they are not different. The difference would be between the different communities of theorists guided by their respective philosophies. Within a community there would be differences (which generate varieties), when each researcher or a group of researchers carry out "research with focus priorities" according to the interests, values or principles of the researcher.

Fourth, regarding the cognitive content or domain of these sets, are pedagogical theories and laws different from didactic theories and laws? How many Didactic laws and Didactic scientific theories can we recite that are different from those of Pedagogy? What is known is that there are no Didactic laws (although certain authors ventured to establish didactic laws as equivalent to pedagogical laws, discussed and analyzed by E. Hashimoto, 2006). In Didactics there are many models that constitute part of its technological theories. Its content is predominantly prescriptive and non-representational propositions. Because these models and these propositions are directed by a utilitarian rationality, as they will serve to transform the teaching-learning or educational teaching process. This can be seen in the lines of research that theorists suggest for the Didactics of experimental sciences. For example, R. Porlán Ariza(1998, p. 179) described:

> *The relationship established by Linn (1987) on priority lines of research is now classic, and has served as an obligatory point of reference for subsequent reworkings, especially in the Anglo-Saxon world. Specifically, this author proposes, among other minor ones, the following basic problems for the development of Science Didactics: a) identify new goals in science teaching; b) develop and refine our knowledge of current teaching and instruction; c) develop and test alternative experimental curricula; d) evaluate the effectiveness of these innovations; e) develop and evaluate new methodologies to estimate student learning; and f) design and evaluate new teacher training models for science teaching.*

> *Of equal interest, even though it does not include the diversity of lines that actually exist, is the synthesis made by Astolfi and*

Develay (1989), referring to the contributions of other authors such as Host (1978) and Tiberghien (1985), a synthesis that is quite representative of existing concerns in the French-speaking world. These authors establish four fundamental areas of research: a) research regarding the construction and evaluation of an alternative didactic model; b) research on disciplinary content, leading to curricular research; c) research on science teaching methods, articulating the epistemological, psychological and social interaction dimensions (studies of student representations, problem-solving learning, etc.); and d) research on classroom organization in relation to specific innovative proposals.

As can be read in the aforementioned quote, what predominates are technological lines of research: developing curricula, teaching methods, classroom organization, disciplinary content, training models, etc., topics that constitute a field of action almost exclusively for Technology. So, the difference in this component is not because there is different scientific knowledge, but because Pedagogy generates scientific knowledge and Didactics generates knowledge of a different type.

All this information and arguments make it very difficult to believe that Didactics is an autonomous science of Pedagogy. Maintaining this position does not withstand the epistemological analysis carried out. Another theoretical position will be analyzed below.

3.3 IS DIDACTIC ART, TECHNIQUE AND SCIENCE?

There are very few theorists who state that Didactics is art, technique and science at the same time; among them is C. Álvarez de Zayas (2004, p. 32), who points out:

The author is convinced that Didactics is [...] art, technology and science. The first is a consequence of highlighting the personal creativity of the person who carries out the teaching task; The second is the result of being consistent with duly established procedures [...] Didactics is a science because it has its own object of study that identifies it as such and also its own methodology.

C. Álvarez de Zayas (2004) intends to talk to us about the multifaceted conception of Didactics, however, in the same quote we find the answer: Didactics as a discipline is not art, art is in the one who carries out the work of teaching. , art is applicable to human achievement. The aim of turning Didactics into something multifaceted is not new. The same thing happened to Pedagogy, and we believe that it has been demonstrated that beyond being a virtue, it is a defect.

Mª Luisa Sevillano García (2011) also pointed out (the message that requires analysis was highlighted in bold).

Currently the concept of Didactics surpasses the etymological meanings related to the art of teaching. The most widespread conceptualization integrates other very important visions and perspectives such as theoretical, technological and practical. All of them make up the new framework of Didactics. Likewise, it is confirmed that teaching as an object of Didactics is not sufficient either and thus the field of learning has also become a formal object of its reflection. (p.8)

Thus, current Didactics must go much further, it must not be content with only transmitting content and information, it requires the ability to construct and reconstruct knowledge, that is, promote autonomy. It should help students build a positive, critical and creative attitude towards life. (p. 23

In this quote, Sevillano expresses the current characteristics of Didactics: theory, technology and art; but he also points out that delving into science is nothing more than a wish, an aspiration, but not a reality that needs to be analyzed.

But Miguel A. Zabalza Beraza (2007) gives the answer to the attempt to convert Didactics into science, technique and art, when he pointed out:

Opponents of Didactics positions usually state in their teaching projects that 'Didactics is the science and art of teaching'. An overly presumptuous phrase that, of course, leaves the issue unresolved. (p. 492)

We began the previous point by pointing out that University Didactics was, in the usual manuals, "the science and art of teaching." But it is a somewhat schizophrenic definition and less explanatory than it should be. What is teaching and its knowledge, an art or a science? Can an activity be science and art at the same time? (p. 494)

By maintaining that Didactics is art, science and technique, once again the mistake of confusing discipline as such, with the exercise of that discipline, just as Álvarez de Zayas does. The nature of the discipline and the way in which the discipline is applied or operates are confused. There is no difference between the discipline itself and the way it is carried out; The first is in the field of knowledge, the other in the operational field. What is important to define is what is (Didactics)? And not how to do it?

The arguments presented to settle the all-embracing character of Pedagogy developed in the chapter On the nature of Pedagogy serve to settle the all-embracing character that some theorists attribute to Didactics. So the conclusion is the same: Didactics cannot be Art, Technique, and Science in the same historical space – time. Also, remember the carpenter metaphor.

3.4 IS DIDACTIC A PART OF PEDAGOGY, AND THEREFORE SCIENCE?

Since 1922 it was already commented that Didactics was part of Pedagogy, V. Pertusa, A. Gil (1922, p. 5) stated, Didactics "we can define it as the part of Pedagogy that has as its object the application and adaptation of the general principles of the science of education to particular cases, that is, to the demands of each student, for their greater and easier improvement."

More recently, F. Larroyo (1963, p. 218) stated, "Didactics is that part of Pedagogy that describes, explains and substantiates the most appropriate and effective methods to lead the student to the progressive acquisition of habits, techniques, knowledge, in short, to his methodical and comprehensive training."

The same J. Aguirre Cárdenas (1995, p. 4) stated:

Pedagogy is the science of education, as a generalized fact integral to the formation of man. Didactics is the science of teaching as a particular fact. Just as teaching is part of education, Didactics is part of Pedagogy. [...] Thus, Didactics, as a consequence of the analysis of the factors that define it, applies methods for teaching and the methods use different techniques to practice them.

Currently, Homero Fuentes (2000), a Cuban intellectual, pointed out that:

Didactics is the science that aims to train professionals, which is expressed through functions, contradictions, categories and laws. [...]. There are General Didactics and special Didactics. ***The first deals with the conception, structuring, and development of the process in the most general aspects..*** *The second deals with the process in particular sciences, technologies or arts. Today we begin to understand the need for knowledge of Higher Education Didactics,* ***since the effectiveness, efficiency, efficiency***

and quality of the training of professionals depends to a large extent on it. *On which social, scientific, cultural, political and educational development will rest.*

Miguel A. Zabalza Beraza (2007)

In summary, current Didactics is that field of knowledge, research, theoretical and practical proposals that focus on the teaching and learning processes: how to study them, how to put them into practice in good conditions, how to improve the entire process. (p. 493)

As a science of the pedagogical field, *Didactics must provide the necessary knowledge to carry out the design and implementation of valuable "didactic acts."*

This practical sense of Didactics, which had been lost, in part, with the construction of abstract and general discourses (on training, on the curriculum, on ideologies or paradigms), is, however, one of its signs of identity. Also, it is fair to recognize it, one of the points of doctrinal disagreement among specialists. (p. 499)

These authors, who come from Mexico, Cuba and Spain, maintain that Didactics is a branch of Pedagogy. Since Pedagogy is a science, then Didactics, as its branch, is science. If we accept this assertion, we conclude that Didactics is a part of Pedagogy, which is born from it, it is a portion of it, just as a biological branch is born from the trunk. Being a branch, it is part of the tree, but it is not a different tree. Just as the locomotive system of the human being, fulfilling an important function, continues to be part of him, this does not mean that it constitutes an autonomous, essentially different being. Didactics would be similar to Statics for Physics, or Organic Chemistry for Chemistry, or Genetics for Biology. Algebra, arithmetic, etc., are branches of Mathematical science, and have no claim to be sciences different from it, until now.

These conceptualizations give us a first major conclusion: If Didactics is a scientific discipline of Pedagogy, a branch of Pedagogy, a part of it, then, the **DIDACTIC IS NOT AN AUTONOMOUS SCIENCE**, but a science dependent on Pedagogy, a science that studies a specific field of Pedagogy. This, of course, if Didactics as a discipline met the requirements demanded of any body of knowledge to be considered a science. I emphasize the condition of subordinate science to the extent that it meets all the requirements that a discipline requires to be scientific. A priori it is accepted, in order to continue studying it.

By accepting a priori that Didactics is part of Pedagogy, the veracity of that assertion remains to be demonstrated. An attempt will be made to establish whether they have the same nature - the fact of being scientific or not - since if they were not, the claims that Didactics is a science, and therefore equivalent to Pedagogy, would be refuted. These reflections present us with a series of academic challenges ahead that we will try to meet, and thus achieve beneficial clarification for the Science of Education. Let's begin by analyzing the "probable" equivalence between Didactics and Pedagogy, and we will continue by explaining whether Didactics is a science.

To achieve a better understanding of this conclusion, a tool provided by mathematical logic and mathematics will be used as an auxiliary tool. This theoretical instrument is the Euler/Venn diagram. To begin the analysis we start from the quote started in this item, where Didactics is considered as part of Pedagogy. To graph this concept, Figure No. 4 is proposed. Do you agree that this figure adequately represents this proposal?

Figure Nº 4 Didactics part of Pedagogy

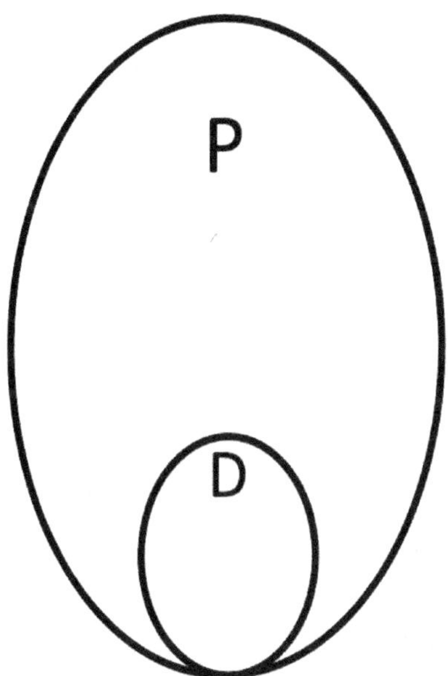

This figure shows us that there is a set P, which contains another set D. Adapting this graph and its conception to Pedagogy and Didactics, it would show that Didactics is not only dependent, but is also part of Pedagogy. At first glance, two sets are observed: Didactics (D) included or contained in Pedagogy (P); Mathematically, a set "D" is said to be included in the set "P," if only if all the elements of "D" are also elements of the set "P."

If we apply this mathematical rule to Pedagogy and Didactics, beyond the empty statements or good intentions of theorists, it forces us to demonstrate that each element of the whole of Didactics must correspond to the whole of Pedagogy. In this demonstration process, the tasks to be carried out are: identify the fundamental elements of each set or discipline, and then compare each of them.

To continue with the reasoning, what common elements between Pedagogy and Didactics can be used to contrast them?

They are proposed, in the first instance: the purpose, objective, contents and methods of each of them (it will no longer analyze the object of study, the community that has been touched on in previous paragraphs). But, before beginning the analysis of the components, we will establish some concepts that will be used as a theoretical foundation.

Beyond the opinion of well-known epistemologists such as M. Bunge, Karl Popper, etc. that deal with the differentiation of science with other types of knowledge, such as technological knowledge, for example, we will emphasize transcribing quotes from dialectical materialist intellectuals, so that they are not branded as "positivist" and other names or adjectives with which they are used. Could try to obscure the argument. For example, Jorge Núñez J. (1999, p. 16), at the time he wrote the book he was Director of postgraduate studies at the University of Havana, a prominent and contemporary representative of the philosophy of science in Cuba, states the following :

> *Let's say to begin that the concept of science is usually defined in opposition to that of technique, according to the different functions they perform. In principle, the function of science is linked to the acquisition of knowledge, to the process of knowing, [...] The function of technique is linked to the realization of procedures and products, to making, whose ideal is usefulness. Technique refers to operational procedures useful from a practical point of view for certain purposes.*

Jaime Breilh (1994. p. 15), an Ecuadorian intellectual with a clear Marxist tendency, cited by Arturo Campaña in the cover sheet of Breilh's book, states that his "scientific approaches, embodied in disciplined intellectual work, are substantiated by [...] the indisputable value of historical materialism, dialectics and scientific socialism" and called him "a fighter [...] alternate president of the Pichincha committee for solidarity with Cuba," he noted:

Science and technology constitute two closely related aspects of knowledge, but substantially different in terms of their content and possibilities. Science produces knowledge, discovering and explaining the essential regularities of the processes to transform them, technology, for its part, applies knowledge produced by adapting it to achieve practical purposes.

In science, the way the subject relates to the object is the method, a way of thinking about reality when acting on it. In technique, the path is the stable procedure or process of successive steps to produce a practical end (p.120).

It is important that we permanently remember these differences as they will help us establish the nature of Pedagogy and Didactics. To facilitate the analysis, table No. 3 is presented (extracted from table No. 2).

Table № 3 Some differences between Science and Technology

Criterion	Characteristics of Science	Technology Features
Purpose	Science seeks laws and theories to describe and explain reality	Technology seeks the production of things, to control and transform certain sectors of reality.
Content	The body of knowledge contains hypo-deductive propositions, it generates specific representational knowledge.	The body of knowledge is normative, regulatory propositions, operational knowledge.
Type of problem addressed	Cognitive problems about concrete/abstract natural and social phenomena	Practical problems referring to artificial and concrete facts
Final product	Knowledge. The relative truth of knowledge is an end and a means	Artifacts, action plans, things or objects. The truth is a means.
Evaluation criterion	Knowledge subject to ethical evaluation (true or false)	Artifacts or objects subject to efficiency and effectiveness criteria.
Social impact	Science is not harmful to society.	Technology can be beneficial or harmful to society.
Type of good produced	Generally it is a cultural and public good	It is a cultural asset and it is always a commodity.
Research method	M. Rational, M. Dialectic, M. Hermeneutic	M. of Scientific Research
Way of approaching the investigation	Problem, hypothesis, contrast hypotheses	Problem-need, select solution, experiment, develop the artifact, evaluate it
Dominant process	Analytical	Synthetic
Workspace	Generally in scientific laboratories	Generally in the field and industrial laboratories.

Reaffirming the differences that exist between scientific and technological knowledge, JK Gilbert (1995, p. 364) has pointed out:

> *Some differences between scientific and technological knowledge based on various characteristics of each: purpose (explanation vs. manufacturing), interest (natural vs. artificial), method (analytical vs. synthetic), procedure (simplification of the phenomenon vs. complexity of the artifact) and result (generalizable knowledge vs. particular and concrete object). These features might seem useful in highlighting differences between science and technology; However, currently both are not totally independent, with such different objectives, methods and products.*

Based on the concepts of Didactics written in the previous paragraphs, the proposed components will be analyzed to establish the character or nature of Didactics, for this purpose as a source of contrast, table No. 3, and what was proposed by Gilbert. Let's analyze:

1. In the description of Didactics, intellectuals First they qualify Didactics as a science, but then they say:

- Larroyo: "...**drive** to the educator to the progressive acquisition of habits, techniques, knowledge."
- Aguirre: "...**apply** methods for teaching and the methods use different techniques to practice them."
- Homer: "**...**since the effectiveness, efficiency, efficiency and quality of the training of professionals depends to a large extent on it."
- Alvarez: "..."It is a systemic, efficient pedagogy."
- Medina: "Didactic knowledge,... performed with efficiency and effectiveness." ""contributed to... optimization, effectiveness, efficiency, quality, control, regulation, etc" "prescribes the training action..."

Now, this use of verbs on the teleological level corresponds to a system of practical knowledge, or as Francine Best would say, theoretical-practical system (currently the known theoretical-practical system is technology). In any case, technology uses the verbs "conduct," "apply," "be efficient, effective." Science uses verbs: describe, explain, predict. These verbs give special functions to each of them, to Didactics that of operating, acting on the teaching-learning process or educational teaching process to improve it, and Pedagogy is assigned the role of knowing, knowing, that and other processes. Science describes, explains and predicts. Science does not apply, it does not lead, it is not efficient or effective, these activities correspond to technology, not science (see the evaluation criteria in the table).

Here there is a first big difference, regarding the purposes: Didactics "leads", "applies," "operates efficiently." Pedagogy "describes," "explains" and "predicts" with truth.

2. The second difference occurs in the contents. Since Didactics must "apply" certain knowledge, the content is predominantly composed of prescriptive, regulative, procedural propositions, which are reflected in norms, rules, methods, strategies, techniques, plans. A. Medina Rivilla (2007, p. 435) himself explicitly states that didactic knowledge prescribes training action. Another example, Francisca Martín Molero (1999) develops a didactic model, which is a:

Model for the functional design of a teaching program is reflected in figure 8.1. [...] The first phase of decision-making and integrated organization of the program design includes the four parameters or elements that the Complutense University requires of all the programs of its centers: objectives, contents, methods and bibliography" (p. 248)

The aforementioned figure 8.1 indicates three phases: planning, process and results. In the first phase are the elements to plan. In the second, the didactic interaction teacher-students-environmental context. In the third phase, analysis of the results, reports and innovative measures. In short, a model that explains how to proceed, a purely technological act.

Since Pedagogy must "explain", the dominant or exclusive body of knowledge is of a display, representational type and is specified in concepts, laws and theories.

Therefore, the second difference between Pedagogy and Didactics is regarding the content. The content of Didactics is a system of rules, generally normative propositions or prescriptions, of a practical nature. The dominant content of Pedagogy is representational, explanatory propositions.

3. The third difference occurs when the aim is to assess the content and purpose of Pedagogy and Didactics. Antonio Medina Rivilla (2007) puts it this way:

Technology is the theory of technique and the systematization and application of scientific knowledge to effectively solve society's problems.

[...]. The technological vision is one of the most valued concepts in 21st century society and is characterized by its applied approach, its commitment to effectiveness and efficiency and the rigor provided by the scientific base and quality action. (p. 432)

In light of the description of the Didactic theorists themselves, What she does is valued as "effective", "effective", "efficient" and "quality", these evaluation criteria are for the functioning of artifacts, processes, strategies, plans. It would be totally wrong to say that a concept or theory is efficient or effective. It is more appropriate to say that this strategy, that plan is more efficient, is more effective or is more effective than another; These evaluation criteria are specific to a technology. The evaluation criteria of science are alethics (true or false), which is why it is said that the concept, theory or law discovered is true or false. It is so inappropriate to say that a strategy or an artifact or a procedure is true or false. From the use of evaluation criteria it is easy to identify whether a proposition (or set of propositions) belongs to science or technology.

If we continue analyzing the components of Pedagogy and Didactics using the components indicated in table No. 3, we could abound in arguments to establish the difference between them.

Considering the three components already stated, the first conclusion could be reached: The Didactics set has some elements that are different from the elements of the Pedagogy set. The second conclusion that comes as a consequence: Pedagogy**it does not have**to Didactics, since there are elements of Didactics not contained in Pedagogy. Didactics is not a subset or branch of the same species, that is, scientific, as Pedagogy. Therefore, the equivalence between Pedagogy and Didactics, in its scientific nature, is being questioned.

4. If we use mathematical language, as another contrast mechanism, it forces the Pedagogy and Didactics set to comply with the reflective, symmetrical and transitive relationship. The first relationship (reflective) requires that all the elements analyzed, for example, the purpose of Didactics and the purpose of Pedagogy, are equal; the content of Pedagogy and the content of Didactics are the same, etc., if it was demonstrated that this is not the case, then it eliminates the possibility of mathematical equivalence.

Let's give an example from real life that, without being at all rigorous, will help clarify this concept. Let's imagine that we are talking about animals, and we want to classify them (read laws or types of science). We want to distinguish cows from horses, goats, donkeys, etc. The first thing we do is define the properties that, indisputably, define a cow and distinguish it from other animals. Accordingly, we do it. We also proceed with goats, horses, etc. When the relationship allows us to identify cows among themselves but distinguish them from other types of animals, etc., we will have a relationship of equivalence. Two elements of the set "animals" will be cows if they meet a series of basic attributes. And they are cows and not goats, because the difference has been perfectly established, and the different types of animals that we contemplate as well as all their characteristics have also been established.

That is, an equivalence relation defines the way to distinguish one type of element from another type of element, such that elements of the same equivalence class are essentially the same, but completely and distinguishably different from elements of the other classes of equivalence. Equivalence: this leads to formalizing the concept of classification. In this way, the concept of equivalence demonstrates that Pedagogy and Didactics, since they do not contain the same elements, are not equivalent, that is, they do not share the same scientific nature.

To the extent that this item has been developed, I believe, the logical and epistemological difficulty of Didactics being a subset or equivalent of Pedagogy is being established. All these arguments have sought to establish that Didactics is not a scientific branch of Pedagogy, they are of a different nature.

3.5 WHAT RELATIONSHIP DOES PEDAGOGY HAVE WITH DIDACTIC?

Now, let's propose a new situation that will be shown in figure 3. This figure would show us a more common case among the sciences. It shows us two sets or sciences that have elements that relate them, a common space where elements that belong to them coexist; but the presence of spaces with totally different elements is also expressed. It is surely these last spaces where the core or essence of each discipline lies.

Figure Nº 5 Disciplinary interaction

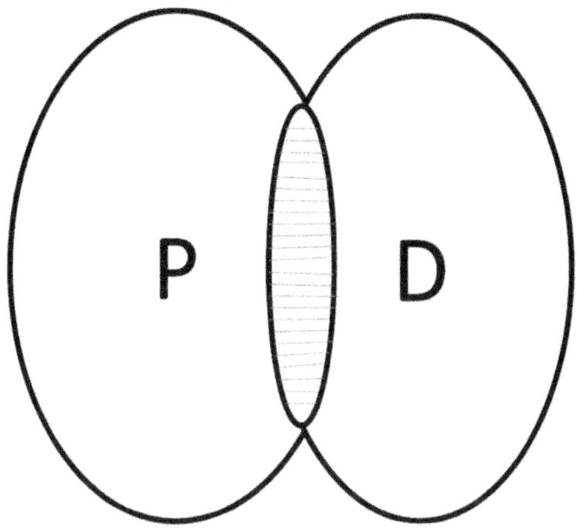

The figure shows the existence of a set "P" different from the set "D", but which marginally contains certain common elements, the space of overlapping disciplines. If we accept that P (Pedagogy) and the set D (Didactics) are sciences, it forces us to accept that they are two different sciences with some common elements. Since they are two sciences that deal with the same object of study, with the same problems and perspective, then one of them is superfluous (as was demonstrated when the autonomous science nature of Didactics was discussed).

The other interpretation would be that set P is a scientific discipline and set D is a discipline of a different nature, for example a technological discipline. If that were the case, the interaction between a scientific discipline and a technological discipline would be easily acceptable, since they could address the same object of study, but they would do so with different problems and with different perspectives.

3.6 IS DIDACTIC TECHNOLOGY?

Just as there are theorists who maintain that Didactics is science, there are others who establish that Didactics is technology. Below we will present a series of concepts about Didactics reviewed by prominent specialists on the subject, whose useful content for the study will be highlighted in bold.

N. Abbagnano, and A. Visalberghi, (1992, p. 204) point out that:

> *Juan Enrique Alsted (1588-1638), professor of philosophy at the University of Herborn and German editor of the work of Giordano Bruno, whom he had learned to admire through the Wittemberguese disciples of the Nolano, also composed a Didactic that he incorporated into a great Encyclopedia. "Didactics," he writes, "is nothing more than the method of study and is equally necessary to all those who study, just as the navigator needs the nautical chart, the architect needs the square and the compass, and the traveler needs the milestone."*

For Alves de Mattos (1963) Didactics is thepedagogical discipline of a practical and normative nature that has as its specific objective the technique of teaching. Defined in relation to its contents,Didactics is the systematic set of principles, standards, resources and specific procedures that serve the learning of content according to educational objectives..

Paciano Fermoso (1982, p. 22, 23), Professor of Theory and History of Education at the Autonomous University of Barcelona, pointed out that: The technical knowledge of education is Didactics, School Organization [...] Technical knowledge Regarding education, in terms of knowledge, it enjoys the same characteristics of all technical knowledge; These are: application of scientific knowledge, practical and concrete way of knowing, beneficial realization of what is scientific and functional intentionality.

MC Vera (1987) states that the concern of Didactics from the humanistic point of view is to focus on **facilitating the acquisition of attitudes**, making the human dimension the only configuring center of the teaching-learning process. But,**from the technical point of view** where the teaching-learning process constitutes an intentional, systematic action, its concern is constituted by aspects such as instructional objectives, teaching strategies, evaluation, etc. In short, it is the enhancement of the objective and rational part of the process.

R. Cervantes (1996, p.9) pointed out "the **Didactics is the practical aspect of Pedagogy** that is supported by a scientific theory"

Iván Bedoya, and Mario Gómez (1997, p. 44 and 45), summarize it this way:

***The technical knowledge of education**[...] It is understood as the application of scientific knowledge: it would be the efficient or active aspect of pedagogical practice [...] But even so, what is interesting in this technical knowledge is not so much knowledge, that is, developing a knowledge, how to make, carry out and operate a process following certain procedures to obtain certain results.*

***This technical knowledge about education is "didactics.""**. With what theoretical body does didactics organize, structure, and operate the teaching-learning process? Didactics is based on the theoretical body of Pedagogy and other sciences to organize, structure and improve the educational teaching process, and produces prescriptive formulations rather than demonstration, regulative rather than explanatory.*

Jaime Fayad and Javier Fayad (2007, p. 57) pointed out that "Didactics is the exercise of a technology, which Michael Foucault defines as 'technology of the self', it is an exercise in which we want to expand the field of learning. Of the individual, through regulated and systematized steps in favor of a product that defines learning."

Antonio Medina Rivilla (2007), referring to the technological perspective of Didactics, because he also points out that it has a scientific perspective, declares:

Didactic knowledge is generated, in this perspective, as rigorous, planned knowledge and doing, carried out with efficiency and effectiveness and valued for its coherence and adjustment to the scientific framework and the intended teleology.

Didactic technology *has contributed to the conception and training practice the terms of systematization, optimization, effectiveness, efficiency, quality, control, regulation, feedback, etc., aiming for the permanent improvement of the practice and the use of resources, generalizing the most positive aspects of the know and do, for the benefit of each human being and society as a whole. (p. 432)*

Didactics has among its approaches the technological one, which prescribes the training action, supported by scientific knowledge. (p.435)

TE Zeitler (2010, p. 4) points out:

In summary: the fundamental difference, as Susana Barco (1989) points out, between the didactics of the 17th and 18th centuries and those of the 20th century lies in the fact that the former are normative, while the latter are only prescriptive: the normative tends to legislate, to impose a purpose without consensus, while the prescriptive is based on customary principles, and functions as a flexible guide and orientation; it does not impose, it recommends; It does not demand, it proposes.

Agustín de la Herrán, quoting Félix E. González Jiménez (2012, p.628), pointed out: "Didactics is the system of communicating knowledge to students who in turn have to do it." In other words: Didactics must promote personal construction from and for knowledge. (Taken from A. de la Herrán, J. Paredes, C. Moral Santaella. and T. Muñoz, 2012).

There is no doubt that for these authors Didactics is Technology. But what is technology?

There are many concepts about technology. In Peru, the official concept is provided by the glossary of Law 28303, which is the Framework Law of Science, Technology and Technological Innovation, it is stated that technology "is an ordered set of instruments, knowledge, procedures and methods applied in different industrial branches to achieve a specific objective, generally that of producing and distributing a good or service", it is good to note that this concept has been extracted from the Frascati Manual published by the OECD in 1994.

J. Ortega y Gasset (1968) pointed out that there were three expressions of the technique:

The empirical technique is that generated temporarily by the demands of life itself.

The craftsman's technique is the set of knowledge and procedures that the craftsman uses to produce a homemade artifact.

The technique of the technician is the set of knowledge and procedures based on mass production (this last type is the one that resembles technology, at that time the term technology was not used)

From this point of view, technology is an expression of technique with certain special conditions.

M. Bunge (1981, pp. 206-207) points out that:

> *Technology is a body of knowledge, if and only if: it is compatible with contemporary science and controllable by the scientific method, and it is used to control, transform or create natural or social things or processes. Technologies can be material (engineering, agronomy, etc.), social (psychiatry, administration, didactics, etc.), conceptual (computing), general (theory of linear systems, control, etc.)*

M. Quintanilla (2005) gives a more complex vision of technology, and manifests concepts depending on the perspective or approach:

> *Cognitive approach: Technology is applied scientific knowledge, which has an industrial application (p.47)*

> *Instrumental approach: It is constituted by the products or results and not by the knowledge on which they are based, that is, it is constituted by the set of industrial artifacts (p. 48)*

> *Systemic or praxiological approach: Technology is a system of actions that include artifacts and acting capabilities based on scientific knowledge, intentionally oriented to the transformation of specific objects to efficiently achieve an objective that is considered valuable (pp. 51, 56)*

From all the concepts presented, it can be concluded that technology is related to "doing" based on science, with the production of industrial artifacts that will serve to transform a reality, a concept that originated with the actions of Galileo, by incorporating the experiment as an associative method of science and technology, theory and practice. Its nature is linked to the production of particular objects that must be adapted to certain circumstances; it is utilitarian in contrast to science, which is theoretical.

However, not everyone accepts these differences, sometimes

the philosophical perspective contributes to confusing technology with science, for example orthodox positivism in its reductionist desire and subordination of technology to science, associated applied science with technology. Marxism, who teaches that science and technology are part of the same process, and that this entire process is called science, so research to obtain knowledge is incomplete if it does not serve to transform reality. And the followers of M. Heidegger who consider that Science is the same as Technique. Or also because of the little progress, at a certain time, of the Philosophy of Technology, as is the case of M. Bunge who in 1966 wrote the essay Technology as an applied science, but as the Philosophy of Technology developed, he modified his opinion. , almost 22 years later, as observed in the book Science: its method and its philosophy, written in 1988 (cited below).

3.7 WHY DIDACTIC IS TECHNOLOGY?

When Didactics began as an educational discipline, it was considered an art, the "art of teaching." It was a practice, generally dependent on the talent and ability of the "didactic" to transmit content when teaching. Sometime later, with the desire to standardize the teaching process and not depend only on the individual talent of the teacher, rules and procedures were established. With the passage of time, with the contribution of other sciences, Education was better understood, and the disciplines that studied it were reconceptualized, among them, Didactics, which expanded its object of study, explicitly incorporated learning. From the original "teaching" it moved to the "teaching-learning process". He also modified his behavior, he went from mechanically applying techniques and procedures to creating new strategies and procedures based on the knowledge that Educational Psychology or Pedagogy gave him.

Currently, due to the systemic nature that dominates modern

thinking, or the influence of the systemic paradigm, the object of study continues to be the teaching-learning process but incorporates into the analysis the study of other educational components (organization, policies, etc.) for purposes to study their interaction and influence on the teaching-learning process. Furthermore, it surpassed its stage of being a recreator of techniques and procedures to become a reflective and operating discipline, a theoretical-practical discipline, that is, it generates new concepts and technological theories that allow it to explain its object of study in order to modify it to make quality training of the person.

The theoretical-practical characteristic of any discipline, including Didactics, is a sui generis characteristic, recently developed, epistemologically, it falls within the spectrum of knowledge of technology. Formerly, the spectrum of knowledge included Theology and Philosophy, then science and technology were incorporated (the latter was only considered a mere application of procedures), and lately Technology. Technology is not science but it uses it as its foundation; science that is adapted to the technological context. It is not an empirical or artisanal technique (to use Ortega y Gasset's classification), but it is its concrete expression.

Didactics due to the purpose it has as a discipline, due to the dominant type of knowledge (system of rules, prescriptive propositions, etc.), due to the assessment made of its products or actions (effectiveness, efficiency, impacts), due to the type of problems it addresses, due to the type of final product, etc., it is undoubtedly a technological discipline.

Technology, as a class of Technique, is a discipline that shares propositions of a demonstration or representational type, that is, technological theories that focus on specifically technological topics such as the design, evaluation and construction of technological systems, theories that are useful for being efficient and not because they are true. It also shares prescriptive propositions, regulators of the technique. The graph in figure No. 6 describes this interaction.

Figure No. 6

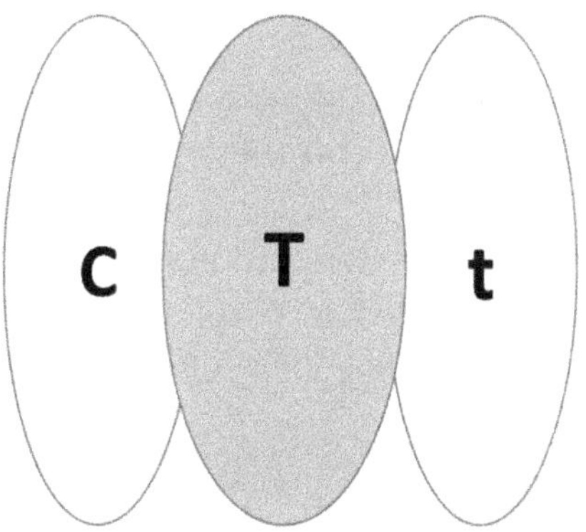

In the figure, set C represents Pedagogy or Educational Science, set T represents Didactics or Educational Engineering, Set T represents the empirical technique or artisanal technique of education, or the practice of the process itself. educational. The figure shows the difference in the sets, this implies that each set has its own elements that characterize them, their natures are not confused. However, intersections are displayed that indicate that these sets share some elements, but that they are the exceptions and not the generality.

Didactics has few propositions of a demonstration type (typical of science) but with a certain directionality, since there are technological theories, which according toJosé A. Acevedo Díaz, Ángel Vázquez Alonso, Mª Antonia Manassero Más and Pilar Acevedo Romero(2003),are:

Technological theory as a body of knowledge that uses systematic experimental methods similar to those of science but focused on the design, construction, behavior and evaluation of technological artifacts and systems. A theory of this type always involves reflection on

*technological practice, which is why it can be considered as a medi-
ator between this and a more abstract scientific theory.*

*Now, it is worth not forgetting that the criterion of validity of a
technological theory is not so much that it is true or plausible but
that it works in practice and is useful, which means distinguishing
between scientific rationality and technological rationality (p.363)*

It also contains rules and procedures to make the action of teaching more efficient. The Didacticsas Technology is for Pedagogy, as Chemical Engineering is for Chemistry or Statistics for Mathematics.

Didactics depends on Pedagogy, its theories, its laws, etc., as well as on other sciences, to explain itself and guide its function. Didactics operates on Pedagogy, it is what is in direct contact with reality itself. If Didactics were the same as Pedagogy, it would no longer have contact with operationalization, norms and procedures. Educational reality tells us that Didactics is the closest thing to educational work. If Didactics is regulated under pedagogical laws and dimensions, in conclusion we will say that Pedagogy protects and guides Didactics with its theory, Pedagogy studies the educational teaching process to explain it, and Didactics studies it to transform it with effectiveness, efficiency and effectiveness.

The definitions of Didactics, its work, the logical and epistemological analysis, the level of the statements, etc., gave us enough arguments, I hope, to help us establish with crystal clarity the character or nature of Didactics. All of this leads us to a conclusion: Didactics is not a science, Didactics is an educational technology, which structures, develops and transforms the teaching-learning process, to enable a student's training process in an efficient, effective and consistent manner. quality.

Didactics is technology, because the teaching-learning process as its object of study that occurs in the training process is studied to transform it. It is technology, because it applies techniques in harmony with the scientific knowledge provided by Pedagogy, Sociology, Psychology, etc., but also reflects on them to improve it or produce something new.

Didactics is technology, because it does not work in isolation, but rather works in a network; that is, through a set of empirical and theoretical knowledge, for a specific purpose. All this discussion does not imply declaring the absolute autonomy of Didactics with Pedagogy, rather they serve to declare their permanent complementation.

Some may criticize for not having a "complex, holistic" vision, where it is understood that science – technique (technology) – production form a complex whole, a unity. I perfectly agree with this last assessment, but it's about being consistent. Let us reflect: this whole is accepted in advance, since the systemic and complex nature of life is not going to be discussed. However, that whole is made up of parts, those parts are different, related, interacted, but in some way different (different in nature, quality or quantity). And if they are different, what we must do is establish the difference, characterize each one. What it is about is distinguishing and not separating. Obviously when studying its interrelationships, it is studied as a whole. This is similar to inter or transdisciplinary studies. First, the characteristics of the disciplines must be differentiated, because these are the basis, and then we can talk about inter- or transdisciplinarity.

But, establishing these differences requires that in addition to investigating and proposing, logical and epistemological work is carried out on the whole but also on its components. On the philosophical level it is possible to treat things as a fan, we have the freedom to reflect openly, in any direction and on any level, analyze and synthesize simultaneously, many things are permissible to us. But, in the field of science and logic especially, the way of approaching matters is more closed, linear, since the idea is to be concrete, where clarity and precision result in the backbones of intellectual work.

3.8 WHAT IS DIDACTIC FOR THE AUTHOR?

In conclusion to everything analyzed, the nature of Didactics is described as **a technological discipline that studies the teaching-learning process both in isolation and in its interaction with other educational components, to make it more efficient and quality in its objective of contributing to the training of the person.**

Stating that Didactics is Technology is neither subordinating it to any science, nor depreciating its value, on the contrary, technology is the support for the development of the world (such as engineering), society (such as administration), education (Didactics). Beyond whether technology does good or harm to humanity, beyond whether science and technology are instruments of liberation or instruments of power, beyond being a way of understanding reality or just tools for action, the "development" of the current civilization is based on it, so much so that many call this historical moment the "age of technology." We could be technophiles or technophobes depending on our ideological location, intellectual power or cultural stratum, we could question or "worship" technology, but what we cannot deny is that modern man has associated his way of life with technology.

3.9 WHY IS IT SO DIFFICULT TO ACCEPT THAT DIDACTIC IS A TECHNOLOGY?

There are several reasons that explain why many members of the educational community do not accept the technological nature of Didactics, these are:

1. Psychological reason.

This reason is brilliantly defined by Félix E. González Jiménez (1990) quoting JC Forquín:

> *Why are teachers particularly reticent about innovations that challenge traditional disciplinary separations? (JC Forquín, 1987), is answered with allusions that range from a certain corporatist sense to a consideration of the defense of what is part of one's own identity. And there may be something to all of this, even a lot, but I think there is more habit and even unconfessed comfort in continuing to do what the system did with them permanently: yes, warning them that it should not be like that" (p.39).*

The reasons given are non-quantifiable reasons, but very weighty. On the one hand, modifying their opinion would imply, for many theorists, losing their own identity. People who were born under the influence of a certain teaching and then tell them that it is a mistake, unconsciously, one tends to defend tooth and nail, even appealing to ad hominen arguments, to devalue the arguments. This is similar in the religious aspect, when a Catholic priest or Protestant pastor is presented with doctrines of another nature, the first thing they do is defend doctrine against doctrine. Feeling that their arguments have no force, they appeal to their "intellectual authority" indicating that they have "A" or "B" academic degrees or have "x" years of experience. And if that does not have an effect, then they attack the person, they confront him with his ignorance, his inexperience, his appearance, etc., finally, they expel him. However, it is good to highlight that contrasting his position, one does not lose identity, but rather gains an improved identity, with fewer errors than before, since one has subjected a theoretical belief to the fire of debate.

Another psychological reason is the influence of what Niestzche called the "Spirit of gravity" or what E. Fromm called the Pathology of Normality, which is the superstitious cult of what is established, the conscious or unconscious promotion of conformism, leading to live in the comfort of an established idea, and anything that disturbs your comfort is psychologically rejected. This is an obstacle that prevents developing science or technology. Scientific truths that in medieval times were considered absolute, later due to the influence of mathematics, became considered exact, today they are accepted to be relative truths. This conclusion should be understood by everyone, truths are not absolute or exact, they are relative and therefore questionable.

This attitude of conformity or of maintaining their scientific "identity" without the corresponding foundations is similar to if the followers of Ptolemy with his geocentric thesis of the universe, currently continued fighting to preserve that thesis, and refused to review or read other proposals. How much reason does this message that circulates on the internet contain:

A Chinese thinker, who lived in the 4th century BC, Chuang Tzu, makes symbolic characters speak, and one of them, whom he calls the God of the North Sea, says: "How can I talk about the sea with the "A frog if he has not left his pond? How can I talk about ice with the summer bird if he is stuck in his station? How can I talk to the wise man about Life if he is a prisoner of his doctrine?"

Message: open our world, our thinking, our rationality for the honest analysis of our beliefs.

2. Sociological reason.

In a lucid and forceful way, Francisca Martín Molero (1999) develops this reason as follows:

It happens, and it happens all too often, that the conjunctural weight of these authors - due to the most diverse circumstances whose clarification is not necessary to analyze here - becomes fashionable. And, with this, they drag not only ideological collaborators, sympathizers and promoters; but to a good part of the scientific community, all the more so the more power the ideology underlying fashion has. And, thus, the ground is fertilized to confuse freely and profusely (p. 101)

In reality, following the teachings of an authority on a certain subject has nothing incongruous or inconsequential, it is the most normal thing, because there are always precursors in that subject, the world does not begin or end with us. What is incorrect, from a scientific point of view, would be that:

1. Instead of responding to a contrary argument with another argument, let us cite the opinion of "our authority" as the basis of our defense. An illustration, cited by someone for whom I do not have the source, goes like this:

It is said that a group of wise men wanted to know the number of teeth a horse had, for this they cited the opinion of Aristotle, others from Plato, others from Anaximander, etc., they analyzed the opinion of each of them and they could not agree. . The boy who had the horse, bored with so many absurd and meaningless speeches, told them: if you want to know the number of teeth on the horse, why don't you open your mouth and count them?

This is what many of us do, instead of resorting to evidence, empirical or rational proof, we resort to the opinion, sometimes unfounded, of authority.

2. There is no doubt that leaders have great influence on the behavior of their followers. But, good education teaches us that we must be lucid and independent enough in our thinking to

question what the authority on the subject whom we admire and respect tells us. The opposite would be to follow the teaching of our leader like "little sheep" or "robots", that would mean being poorly educated. History shows us that there are people or peoples who were "badly educated", for example, when Hitler was leader of the German people and they accompanied him in the Holocaust.

3. Epistemological reason.

This reason explains why many theorists have transformed Didactics from Technology to Applied Science, and therefore find it difficult to modify their beliefs. Many European and American theorists (from the north and south) have described Didactics as a science. To refer to scientific nature, they have called it science, theoretical-practical scientific discipline, applied science, etc. When someone referred to it as technology, it was challenged and questioned. However, everyone agrees that Didactics is a theoretical-practical discipline. The difficulty in accepting such a situation lies in the incorrect use of the word science or applied science. Why do we say it is wrong?

Francisca Martín Molero (1999) helps us understand the epistemological error when she analyzes the character of General Didactics, she says it this way:

Etymologically, technology comes from the Greek techne, which means art, industry [...] and logos, which means study or treatise. Today, applied science, which implies knowing how to do things in accordance with its principles, or the ability guided by reason to act or produce objects and therefore creatively. (p. 104)

Didactics is the science applied to the teaching-learning process with a view to the intellectual and human growth of the subject, through the optimization of said process. (p. 106)

F. Martín is equating technology with applied science. This equalization is the source of confusion in defining the nature of Didactics. And this is a problem of philosophical training.

The same happens with the description of Javier Suso López, and M. Eugenia Fernández Fraile (2001) cited above when they described the characteristics of Specific Didactics:

"Didactics is not a mere technical adaptation of prior linguistic knowledge. Didactics constitutes a 'Theory of application', a 'Technology'; That is, it has an inherent reflective component about its object, which it will establish from the apprehensions and descriptions of linguistic science, like the rest of the applied sciences with respect to the corresponding basic science" (p. 22).

For Francisca Martín Molero and Javier Suso - Mª Fernández "Technology is Applied Science" what does this mean? This is the key to understanding the whole matter. The other authors cited (those who consider Didactics a science), describe Didactics as a "pedagogical discipline", "a systemic (that is, scientific) Pedagogy", "a theoretical-practical discipline", to a certain extent they want to express the characteristic of Didactics as "a science", or "an applied science" which for them is equivalent to a "technology".

What would happen if Technology is not the same as Applied Science? Would the error be accepted and the way of thinking and acting modified? Not knowing how to differentiate Applied Science from Technology is understandable, given that concepts have been distorted since the teacher training processes. Orthodox positivism could have influenced teacher training, where some of its features were to subordinate technique to science, and thereby equate applied science with technology, to leave the basic sciences as science.

To deepen the differences, subtle or significant, between applied science and technology, we will use four different inputs: the opinion of the authorities on the matter, semantic analysis, logical analysis and illustrations of the differences.

a. The opinion of authorities on the matter.

Two first authors recognized in the world have been selected, who first accepted the equality between technology and applied science, but then changed their points of view, due to new reflections on this matter. Then to a third author without the global gravitation of the first two.

- In 1966, M. Bunge wrote the essay Technology as Applied Science (many theorists stayed with this reading), but 22 years later, as observed in the book Science: Its Method and Philosophy, written in 1988 (p. 34 , 35) noted:

But technology is more than applied science in the first place, because it has its own research procedures, adapted to specific circumstances that are far from the pure cases that science studies. Secondly, because every branch of technology contains a wealth of empirical rules discovered before the scientific principles in which – if these rules are confirmed – they end up being absorbed. Technology is not merely the result of applying existing scientific knowledge to practical problems: living technology is, essentially, the scientific approach to practical problems.

Evandro Agazzi (1997), who was previously in favor of equating technology with applied science, said the following in the Seminar "The epistemological impact of technology" at the Faculty of Philosophy of the University of Seville:

*In conclusion, already at the beginning, modern science reveals itself to be structurally connected to technology, since, first of all, it is necessary to invent and build an instrument to "observe" nature; Secondly, the scientific "experiment" consists of the realization of an artificial situation, precisely because only within an artificial situation can what is never seen in a natural observation be brought into view. Thus, experimental science is a science that already, in its birth certificate, has technology written in its roots. [...]. **Therefore, technology is more than applied science:***It is also that, but it also enters, through very deep paths, into the very structure of the knowledge scientist. [...]. Therefore, from an epistemological point of view, technology, through technological products, constitutes the strongest basis for accepting the majority of current scientific theories, and does not only refer to the practical usefulness of its applications.*

- A third opinion that clarifies the difference between Technology and Applied Science is provided by JA Acevedo Díaz (1998, p. 7), when he describes not only the training problems in science teaching, but also establishes the exhaustive difference between technology and applied sciences, by declaring the following:

The vast majority of attempts made to introduce some knowledge of technology into science teaching, from the perspective of science integrated with technology (UNESCO, 1990), have rather contributed to reinforcing a distorted vision of technology hierarchically subordinated to science, or to favor its erroneous identification with applied science.

Other philosophers of science and technology could be cited as drawing the distinction between technology and science, but one could be accused of choosing theorists who defend a position. In the case of Bunge and Agazzi they are special cases, not only because they are respected intellectuals, but because they previously defended a contrary position, and their evolution or change must have obeyed very powerful reasons, to use a lyrical phrase, "the reasons of the truth".

b. From the Semantic point of view.

Science is subdivided, according to its purpose, into basic science and applied science. The substantive is science and the adjective is its purpose. The substantive defines nature, the adjective its accidental characteristic. The substance of a science is to generate knowledge to describe and explain an educational fact.

In the same way - understanding that there are more refined concepts of technology - for didactic reasons, Ortega y Gasset (1968) will be used, who considered three types of technique: the empirical technique, the craftsman's technique and the technician's technique (today technology). We conclude that Technology is a kind of Technique. The substantive is the technique, the adjective is quality or complexity. The substance of a technique is to operate and create objects or artifacts to transform reality and the adjective what type of knowledge it uses.

Conclusion, the difference between science (including applied science) and technology is established. The nature of applied science, being science, its activity is to describe and explain/understand the educational fact, and the nature of Technology, being Technical, its activity is to create artifacts to control and transform reality.

c. From the logical point of view.

Let's apply the principles of logic:

4. The identity principle:

Applying it to our case, let's begin by conceptualizing Didactics as a science:

C: Science, set of theoretical propositions.
T: Technology, set of theoretical-practical propositions.
t: Technique, set of practical propositions.
D: Didactics.

So.

If D is C: and, C is C, then D is C.
If D is C; and, C is not T; So D is not T.
If D is C; and, C is not t, therefore, D is not t.

This analysis demonstrates that if D (Didactics) is science then D is not Technology. The same would be to analyze the possibility that D is Technology, then D is not science. Stating that it is science and also technology is a contradiction, which does not conform to this law.

This analysis is contradicting all those who say that Didactics is Science and is also Technology, unless Applied Science and Technology are the same thing, and it has been proven that this is not the case.

5. The principle of contradiction:

1. The same conditions follow for C is science, T is Technology, and t is technique.
2. We use C as a reference (it could start with any).
3. We accept differences in the nature of different knowledge,

So:

T is not C

t is not C

So; C is not T

C is not you

If we admit that Didactics is science, then Didactics is not Technology or technique. The conclusion of applying these laws is that Didactics is Science or Technology; It would only be Applied Science and Technology if they were equal. Therefore, if it had been demonstrated that Didactics is Technology then we must accept that it is not science or applied science.

d. A fourth entry, are the illustrations developed in subchapter 2.2, item by Mario Bunge and table No. 3 developed by the author; reread that information as another reflection for the analysis.

All this empirical, logical or epistemological evidence, we hope, does not automatically change your points of view, because this would mean an insult to your intelligence and good education, but at least gives you a point of support to change (in the manner of Archimedes), or a point of disagreement to outline their reasoning and develop new arguments that allow them to strengthen their theoretical position. This work of substantiating a position, which does not make me a precursor of an original idea (although some forms of argumentation in education are original), makes me feel like Galileo, who was not the precursor of the Heliocentric Theory of the universe, but which was the one that scientifically substantiated Copernicus's proposal.

FINAL THOUGHTS

Education as a process in a society and in the individual is natural and artificial. In the first case, innatism is explained by biological aspects (to a large extent) and in the second case, by social and cultural contexts. One of the essential characteristics of education is the emotional motivation that begins the educational process. Another is the "tax" nature, of which the power groups have great responsibility for designing, organizing and executing them. Becoming aware of this fact will force those who possess this privilege to rethink the objectives they intend to achieve.

Education must be given purposes, values, a social function, for this it requires that it be studied at a level where science and technology do not reach it. This study is achieved with philosophical investigations, which, taking into account society, the type of person desired can provide the necessary explanations. It also requires theories that explain the educational fact, laws to discern the future educational scenario. For this, scientific research is required. What should we call this field of knowledge? The proposal is that it be called Pedagogy. However, science for science's sake, although enriching, is unproductive. To do so, it is necessary to move to a more concrete level, to relate knowledge to techniques. It is necessary to use science to transform reality, it is required to operationalize science to achieve solutions to multiple problems. This is the field that we propose to be Didactics.

But, given the immense diversity of interpretations of Pedagogy and Didactics, it has generated distortions in educational research at different levels. Miguel A. Zabalza Beraza (2007), indicating the importance of clarifying the concepts and their implication in educational work, referred to it as follows:

> *We began the previous point by pointing out that University Didactics was, in the usual manuals, "the science and art of teaching." But it is a somewhat schizophrenic definition and less explanatory than it should be. What is teaching and its knowledge, an art or a science? Can an activity be science and art at the same time? [...] It may seem like a banal issue or a topic of discussion for opposing candidates. But it's not like that. It is a key issue because depending on the position adopted, our actions as teachers will have a sufficiently stable and predictable character on the one hand (science) or they will appear as activities dependent on the situation, personal style or the particular circumstances that occur at that time. moment (art). In the same way, if everything depends on the will and expertise of each person (art), there is little room for systematic knowledge and a discipline like Didactics would have little to contribute (pp. 494, 495)*

Considering the great importance of being clear about the concepts, about what they really are: Education, Pedagogy and Didactics, since it is the starting point, to describe their content and actions, I allow myself, using the principle of the object character of Vygotsky make a model that allows us to understand the performance of each of these concepts. In figure No. 7 we graph education as a process.

Fig. No. 7

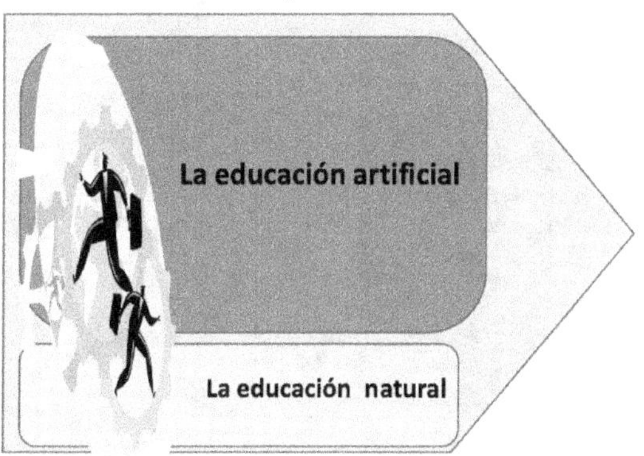

The figure shows that men go through natural education and artificial education to become people with values and goals that their families and society define for them. The figure also shows that they are two processes that historically run in parallel, and that must be objects of attention by power groups (parents, governments at all levels, media, church, etc.)

In these processes, visible or invisible, there are components that configure the processes. The interactions of these components define the type of education. This explains the different types of education that exist in different countries or societies, and in different families. The components are seen in figure 8.

Figure No. 8

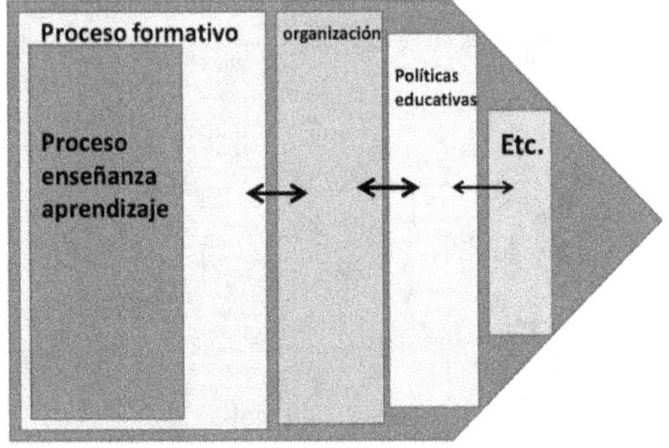

The training process is the most important component of Education, and within it the teaching-learning process. This process is influenced by the interaction with the other components, and by the influence of the environment, since it works as a system. Now, these isolated components or when they interact in a structure in natural or artificial Education, can be studied philosophically, scientifically, technologically or intuitively. The study of education as a system, and the processes as a subsystem, can be seen in Figure No. 9, which shows it as an object of study.

Figure No. 9

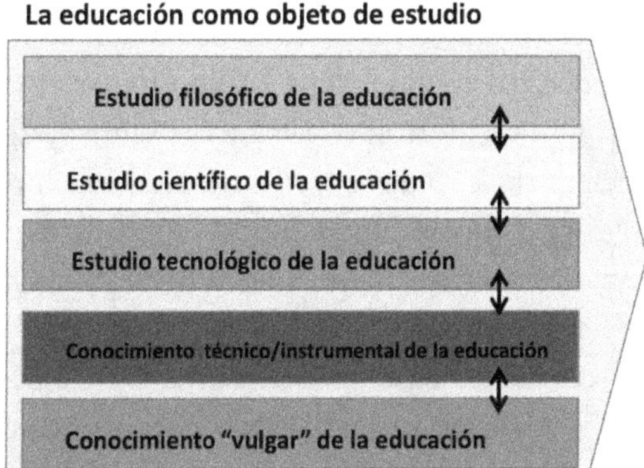

If we make a mental effort and superimpose figure No. 8 with figure No. 9, it shows us that the components or elements of education can be studied from different levels. These studies generate different types of knowledge.

This exhibition allows us to understand and classify the type of research we are going to carry out, otherwise it would be promoting the "Babel" that exists today. If it is intended to carry out a philosophical investigation of some isolated component of education or interacting with other components, then the knowledge generated must predominantly revolve around presenting gnoseological theories, the purposes and values to be developed, in epistemological, logical, ontological, and aesthetic analyses.

If the aim is to develop scientific research on education, as a system or its components in isolation, then the knowledge generated predominantly, at the first level, will be the description of the educational fact, the generation of new concepts or categories; but at a second level, it will require the discovery of a new law or a new model, and a new theory. If the aim is to develop educational technological research, as a system or its isolated components, then the predominant achievements, at the first level, will be the "causal" description of the educational fact. At a second level, it will be the presentation of the solution to the problems raised.

On the other hand, the philosophical, scientific or technological study of education can be carried out by different people, if they have specialized in some field of knowledge, and generates poly or interdisciplinary studies. Or by the same person, if he or she has sufficient skills to do so, generates multiple investigations. The complexity of education merits multidimensional and interdisciplinary study, but respecting and identifying the nature of the disciplines studied and the type of knowledge that is generated. It is necessary to emphasize that there are interactions in each type of knowledge or knowledge, nothing is isolated. The same thing happens in medicine, there are specialists who do basic scientific research, for example genetics. There are specialists who do applied scientific research, there are researchers who do technological research, and also those who only practice the procedures learned at the university or in their daily work.

Regarding Pedagogy, although there is greater consensus, it is not free of contradictions. It was intended to demonstrate that it is the Science of Education, and therefore, it does not belong to the Educational Sciences. It was intended to demonstrate that it is only Science and that it does not constitute Science-Technology-Art. But it was also admitted that it is a science in emergence, an immature science, that works hard through its scientific community to increase knowledge and its specific methods.

Establishing the nature of Didactics was one of the most arduous tasks, due to the different traditions that exist around it: the American, German and French traditions. Also, because there is a large current of opinion that defends the scientific nature of Didactics (as an applied science). We hope that after the logical and epistemological analysis, its technological nature has been fully established.

I hope that those who read this document believe that what is proposed is acceptable because it has been based on a well-founded, rigorous, consistent and reasonable analysis. An acceptable proposal because it is "true" or because its argument has greater explanatory capacity than the other proposals that circulate in the educational noosphere. It would be very sad to believe that this proposal is "true" just because it may be acceptable by the community of educational theorists (applying a descriptive epistemology as a foundation, where the "convention" or consensus of criteria establishes the "truth" of a proposal).By using normative epistemology as an instrument of analysis, the aim is to assume the point of view of scientific rigor, where the minimum required is that its statements be consistent, not contradictory, that it is demonstrated that it is truthful or has or greater capacity. Explanatory than other proposals. The effect of an inconsistency or falsity in part of a theory, applying standard logic, would be to jeopardize the entire theory. If we are careful about our own scientific work, we must be very careful in exposing or accepting statements without having proven their consistency and veracity.

I ask that the proposal be questioned because it is irrational, superfluous, weak, illogical, and not because it does not belong to the "known" circle of scholarship, of the community that "dominates educational thought." That is to say, it would not be correct to subvert the criteria in the arbitration of a proposal: instead of the evidence, physical or rational, the consistency of an argument, determining the character of a reasonable and explanatory proposal, we leave that power to a community of well-intentioned "theorists", but who have their interests, prejudices, values that support a certain paradigm.

BIBLIOGRAPHY

1. Abbagnano N., Visalberghi, A. (1992). History of Pedagogy. Ninth reprint. Translation by Jorge Hernández Campos. Spain: Economic Culture Fund, Branch in Spain.

2. Acevedo Díaz J. (1998). Three criteria to differentiate between science and technology, in E. Banet and A. de Pro (eds.): Research and Innovation in Science Teaching. Vol. I, pp. 7-16. Murcia: DM.

3. Acevedo Díaz JA, Vázquez Alonso Á., Manassero Mas Mª A. and Acevedo Romero P. (2003). Beliefs about technology and its relationships with science Electronic Journal of Science Teaching, Vol. 2, No. 3, 353-376 (2003)

4. Adúriz-Bravo A. and Izquierdo Aymerich M. (2002). About science teaching as an autonomous discipline.Electronic Journal of Science Teaching, Vol. 1, No. 3, 130-140 (2002)130. Barcelona. Taken from thewww.saum.uvigo.eson March 10, 2012.

5. Adúriz-Bravo A. (2001). Integration of Epistemology in the training of science teachers. Doctoral Thesis of the Doctoral Program in Didactics of experimental sciences. Department of Didactics of Mathematics and Experimental Sciences. Autonomous University of Barcelona - Bellaterra.

6. Aguirre Cárdenas J. (1995) Pedagogical Training and University Didactics. Rev. Educational Profiles, April-June, number 68: Mexico: National Autonomous University of Mexico.

7. Álvarez de Sayas Carlos (2004). Didactics of higher education. Lambayeque – Peru: FACHSE Editorial Fund.

8. Álvarez de Zayas, C. (2004). Didactics of Higher Education. Lambayeque-Peru: FACHSE editorial fund.

9. Álvarez Nivia and de la Herrán Agustín (2009). Keys to self-knowledge. Camagüey: Editorial Ácana.

10. Antiseri, D. (1977). Fundamentals of interdisciplinary work. La Coruña: La Coruña.

11. Asensi Díaz J. (2012). (p. 592) Taken from Herrán, A. de la, Paredes, J., Moral Santaella, C. and Muñoz, T. (2012). Fundamental questions of teaching. . 2nd edition. Madrid: Universitas (721 pp.). ISBN: 978-84-7991-362-5.

12. Avanzini, G. (1982), The pedagogy of the 20th century. 3rd ed. Spain: Ediciones Narcea SA Barcelona: Labor.

13. Barrios Graziani L. (2007). Critical vision of post-rationalist theories of education. Venezuela: Central University of Venezuela.

14. Bechelloni Giovanni(1977) From the analysis of the processes of reproduction of social classes and the cultural order to the analysis of the processes of change. Taken from Pierre Bourdieu, Jean Claude Passeron. (1977). The reproduction. Elements for a theory of the education system. Notes on translation. Barcelona: Editorial Laia/Barcelona.

15. Bedoya Madrid JI. (2005). Epistemology and pedagogy: Critical historical essay on the object and pedagogical methods. Sixth edition. Bogotá: ECOE editions.

16. Bedoya, I., and Gómez M. (1997). Epistemology and Pedagogy. Critical historical essay on the pedagogical object and method. Bogotá: ECOE Ediciones.

17. Bermúdez Sarguera R, Rodríguez Rebustillo M. (2003). The activity structure proposed by AN Leontiev could be psychologically inconsistent. Rev. Cuban Psychology. 2003.

18. Best Francine (1988). Avatars of the word Pedagogy. Rev. Perspectives. Vol. XVIII, No. 2, 1988 (66). Paris: UNESCO.

19. Best Francine;Debesse Maurice;Dottrains Robert;Léveque Raphael;Mialaret Gaston(1972). Introduction to Pedagogy. Barcelona: Oikos-Tau.

20. Blanco Rufino (1930). Educational theory. Vol. I. Madrid: Ed. Hernando.

21. Buenfil, Burgos R. (1992). Analysis of education discourses. Mexico: Department of Educational Research Center for Research and Advanced Studies of the National Polytechnic Institute.

22. Bunge M. (1981). Epistemology. Refresher course. Spain: Editorial Ariel.

23. Bunge, M. (1984). Science and development. Buenos Aires. Ed. Twentieth century.

24. *Bunge M. (1988). Science, its method and philosophy. Buenos Aires: Ediciones Siglo Veinte.*

25. Bunge, M. (1999). Validity of Philosophy. Lima: Editorial Fund of the Inca Garcilaso de la Vega University.

26. Bunge M. (2002). Being, Knowing, Doing. Mexico:They co-publish Editorial Paidós Mexicana, SA, and the Faculty of Philosophy and Letters, National Autonomous University of Mexico.

27. Bunge M. (2005). Search Philosophy in the Social Sciences. 2nd edition in Spanish. Mexico: Siglo XXI Editores. Anonymous Society of Variable Capital

28. Bunge M. (2009). Scientific research strategies. Lima-Peru: UIGV Editorial Fund.

29. Camilloni A. de, Davini MC, et al (1995). The Teacher Training in question: Politics and Pedagogy. Buenos Aires: Paidos.

30. Castro Kikuchi L. (2005). Dictionary of educational sciences. Lime.

31. Castro L, and Jorge Fusario R. (1999). Teleinformatics: for information systems engineers. Vol. I. 2nd ed. Barcelona: Editorial Reverté SA

32. ECLAC / Orealc. (1992), Education and knowledge: axis of productive transformation with equity.

33. Cervantes PR (1996). Didactics of Language and Literature. Lima – Peru: Chong Long Editions.

34. Comenio Juan Amós (1998). Great Didactics. Eighth edition. Mexico: Porrúa Editorial.

35. Dámaris Díaz H. (1999). University Didactics: essential reference for quality teaching. Interuniversity electronic journal of Teacher Training, 2 (2). [Available at http:www.uva.es/aufop/publica/revelfop/99-v2n1.htm].

36. Debesse Maurice (1976). Défiaux sciences de l'education?, en L'apport de les sciencies fondamentales aux sciences de l'education. Vol 1. Paris: EPI.

37. Dewey John (1968). The science of education. Translated Lorenzo Luzuriaga. Buenos Aires: Losada.

38. Dewey John (1977). My pedagogical creed. Theory of education and society. Lorenzo Luzuriaga (Trans.) 6th edition. Buenos Aires: Latin American Publishing Center.

39. Díaz Fabelo T. (1958). Critical study of education throughout history. Havana: Publications of the National College of Normal and Equivalent Teachers.

40. Dieguéz Lucena A. (1998) Scientific Realism. An introduction to the current debate in the philosophy of science. Malaga: University of Malaga.

41. Durkheim Émile (1976). Education as socialization, Sígueme Editions, Salamanca.

42. Eder ML and Adúriz Bravo A. (2001). Epistemological approach to the relationships between the Didactics of Natural Sciences and General Didactics. Rev. Tecne, Episteme and Didaxis. Number 9, pp. 2-16. National Pedagogical University.

43. Escolano Agustín (1978). The educational sciences. Reflections on some epistemological problems. In Escolano Sánchez de Zavala,

Fernández Pérez, et al. Epistemology and education. Salamanca: Follow me.

44. Fayad Jaime and Fayad Javier (2007) Taken from María Clara Tovar de Acosta (comp.). Higher education and pedagogy meetings. Cali-Colombia: Universidad del Valle publishing program.

45. Feldman Daniel (2010). General Didactics. Buenos Aires: National Institute of Teacher Training.

46. Beautiful, Paciano. (1985). Educational theory. An anthropological interpretation. Barcelona: CEAC Editions, SA

47. Ferrandez A., Sarramona J. (1980). Differential aspects of education. 2nd ed. Barcelona: CEAC Editions.

48. Follari Roberto (1989). Didactics: epistemological approach. Lectures given at National Didactics Conferences. Argentina: University of San Juan.

49. Foucault, M. (1972). TheArcheologyof knowledge.Mexico: Edit. XXI century.

50. Freire Paulo (2010). Pedagogy of autonomy and other texts. Havana: Editorial Caminos. ISBN: 978-959-303-022-9.

51. Sources Homer (2000). Didactics of Higher Education. Cuba: "Manuel F. Gran" study and higher education center, Universidad del Oriente.

52. García A. Lorenzo (1989). Education: theories and concepts, integrative perspective. Madrid: Paraninfo Editorial.

53. Gautherin Jacqueline (1999).Marc-Antoine Jullien de Paris (1775-1848).Rev. Perspectives Vol. XXIII, nos. 3-4, pp. 805-821. 1993. Paris: UNESCO: International Bureau of Education.

54. Gil Pérez D., Carrascosa Alís J., and. Martínez Terrades F. (1999).The Emergence of Science Teaching as a specific field of knowledge. Education and Pedagogy Magazine. Vol. XI. No. 25 (1999). Medellín - Colombia: University of Antioquia.

55. Gilbert, J. K. (1995). Technology education: a new subject around the world. Science Teaching, 13(1), 15-24.

56. Giroux A. Henry (1986). Beyond the correspondence theory. In "The new sociology of Education", Anthology. Editions el caballito, SEP. Mexico.

57. Gonzales WJ Ed. (2007). The Sciences of Design: Bounded Rationality, Prediction and Prescription. La Coruña - Spain: Netbiblo.

58. González AM (1987). The person-centered approach: Applications to education. Mexico: Editorial Trillas.

59. González Jiménez Félix E. (1990). About the situation and meaning

of Didactics. Complutense Magazine of Education. Vol. I (1), 31-54. Madrid: Complutense University Editorial.

60. González Jiménez Félix E. (2012, p.628), Taken from Herrán, A. de la, Paredes, J., Moral Santaella, C. and Muñoz, T. (2012). Fundamental questions of teaching. 2nd edition. Madrid: Universitas (721 pp.). ISBN: 978-84-7991-362-5.

61. González Jiménez FE, Díez Barrabés M. (2004). Specific didactics: considerations on principles and activities. Complutense Magazine of Education. Vol. 15 No. 1 (2004) 253-286. ISSN: 1130-2496.

62. González, Julia and Wagenaar, Robert. Tuning educational structures in Europe. I. Final report. Bilbao: University of Deusto, 2003. 316 p. Available on the Internet: <http://tuning.unideusto.org/tuningeu/> Accessed on: 02/12/2007.

63. Habermas, Jürgen (2001). Knowledge and interest. Philosophers and their texts. Retrieved on September 20, 2006 fromhttp://usuarios.lycos.es/Cantemar/Conocimiento.html

64. Hashimoto Moncayo Ernesto (2006). Pedagogical laws or pedagogical errors. Cajamarca-Peru: National University of Cajamarca.

65. Herrán, A. de la, Paredes, J., Moral Santaella, C. and Muñoz, T. (2012). Fundamental questions of teaching. Madrid: Universitas (721 pp.). ISBN: 978-84-7991-362-5.

66. Herrán, Agustín de la (1998). Human consciousness, towards a transpersonal education. Madrid: San Pablo.

67. Kerschensteiner G. (1926). Theorie der bildung [theory of education]. Leipzig; Berlin, Taken from Hermannröhrs (1999). Georg Kerschensteiner (1852-1932). Quarterly Journal of Comparative Education. Vol. XXIII. Paris, UNESCO: International Office of Education.

68. Kneller George (1967). Philosophy of Education. Cali (Colombia): Ed. Norma.

69. Konstantinov NA, Mediski EN, Shabaeva MF (n.d.). History of pedagogy. Mexico: Open University. Taken fromhttp://www.universidadabierta.edu.mx.

70. Larroyo Francisco (1963). The science of education. Improved eighth edition. Mexico: Editorial Porrua, SA

71. Latour, B. (1992). Science in action. How to follow scientists and engineers through society. Translated by E. Aibar, R. Méndez and E. Penisio.

72. Lorenzano, Pablo (2000). About the laws in Biology. Rev.Episteme13 (2000). National University of Cordoba.

73. Lungren Ulf P (1981). Curriculum theory and schooling. Spain: Morata Editorial.

74. Marshall James (1994). Foucault and educational research. In SJ Ball (comp.), Foucault and education (2nd ed.). Madrid: Morata Editions.

75. Martín Molero Francisca (1999). Didactics in the face of the third millennium. Madrid. Synthesis editorial. SA

76. Martínez Priego Consuelo (2008). Dialogues on anthropology and education. February – May 2008. Bubok Publishing SL Bubok.

77. Mattos de, Alves (1963). Compendium of General Didactics. Buenos Aires: Editorial Kapeluz.

78. Medina Rivilla Antonio (2007).Technological Vision of Didactics. Contribution of Doctors Fernández Huerta and Rodríguez Diéguez. Rev. Bordón 59 (2-3), 2007, 431-449, ISSN: 0210-5934

79. Morando, Dante (1969). Pedagogy. Critical history of the pedagogical currents that have shaped the development of education. Barcelona: Luis Miracle publishing house.

80. Münsterberg Hugo (1911). Psychology and the teacher.Barnes, Sunday(translator). Madrid: Daniel Jorro.

81. Nassif, R. (1958). General Pedagogy. Buenos Aires: Kapelusz Editorial.

82. Nassif, R. (1980). General Pedagogy. Madrid: Editorial Kapelusz.

83. Niiniluoto, I. (1997). Science versus Technology: Difference or identity? Arbor, 620, 285-299.

84. Núñez Jorge (1999). Science and technology as social processes. What science education should not forget. Havana: Editorial Félix Varela.

85. Organization for Economic Cooperation and Development (OECD) (2003). Understanding the brain. Towards a new science of learning. Antonio Moreno Paniagua (Editorial Management) Sergio Bojalil Parra (Trans.). Mexico, OECD/ Classroom XXI/ Santillana.

86. Ortega y Gasset, José (1968). Meditation technique. Madrid: Western Magazine.

87. Pertusa Périz, V., Gil Muñiz, A. (1922). Modern pedagogy. Volume I. Treatise on Education. 3rd ed. Malaga: Hispaniola.

88. Piscoya Hermoza Luis (1974). On the nature of Pedagogy. Lima: Paper altarpiece, Editions.

89. Ponton Ramos C. (2002). Conceptual constitution of education as an object of study and its impact on the training of professionals in education. Rev. Educational profiles year/vol. XXIV. Numbers 97-98 (pp. 117-126). Mexico: Autonomous University of Mexico.

90. Porlán Ariza R. (1992). The Didactics of sciences. An emerging discipline. Pedagogy Notebooks.

91. Porlán ArizaR. (1998). Past, present and future of science teaching.Science teaching: journal of research and teaching experiences, ISSN 0212-4521,Vol. 16, No. 1, 1998, p. 175-186.

92. Quintana José (1996). Pedagogy or educational sciences? In First International Congress of Epistemology and Education. San José de Costa Rica: UNED Editorial.

93. Quintanilla Miguel A. (2005). Philosophy of Technology, 5 Lessons. Lima: Editorial Fund of the Inca Garcilaso de la Vega University.

94. Rink FT (1803). Immanuel Kant. Pedagogy. (Lessons on pedagogy that Kant gave at the University of Königsberg, and collected by his disciple FT Rink). Poland: ARCIS University School of Philosophy. Taken from thewww.philosophia.cl. accessed June 25, 2010.

95. Ríos Beltrán R. (s/a). The educational sciences. Between universalism and cultural particularism. Ibero-American magazine of education. Taken from thewww.rieoei.org/delos readers/963Rios.PDF. Accessed on May 5, 2012.

96. Robert Paul(s/a) education in Finland: The secrets of amazing success., Translation: Manuel Valdivia Rodríguez. Taken fromwww.otraescuelaesposible.es/PDF/secretos_finlandia/PDF. Accessed on 05/15/2012.

97. Rodríguez Martínez A. (2006). Knowledge of education as a framework for interpreting the Theory of Education as a discipline. Rev. Pedagogical Trends 11. University of Santiago de Compostela.

98. Ruiz Bolívar C. (2008). The multimethod approach in social and educational research: A look from the Complexity paradigm. Journal of Philosophy and Socio-politics of Education: Teré. Number 8. Year 4. 2008. Venezuela:Simón Rodríguez National Experimental University.

99. Samaja, J. (1999). Epistemology and methodology. Elements for a theory of scientific research. Third edition. Buenos Aires: Eudeba.

100. Yesanmartí, N., and Pujol, RM (2002). What does "training for action" entail within the framework of the school?, in Research in School nº 46. Pp49-55, Seville.

101. Savater Fernando (1997). The value of educating. Barcelona: Ariel Publishing.

102. Sevillano García Mª Luisa (2011). Didactics at the core of Pedagogy. Rev. Pedagogical Trends No. 18. 2011.

103. Suarez D. Reynaldo (1995). Education: its Philosophy, its Psychology, its Method. 10th Reprint. Mexico: Editorial Trillas.

104. Suso López J., Fernández Fraile ME (2001) The Didactics of the Foreign Language: Analysis and assessment of the Spanish curriculum for communicative teaching/learning of the FL. Granada: Editorial Comares.

105. Toulmin Stephen (1977). Human understanding. Vol. 1: The collective use and evolution of concepts. Madrid: Editorial Alliance.

106. Touriñán López JM (1987). Educational theory. Madrid. Ed. Anaya.

107. Touriñán López JM (1989) Pedagogical Knowledge: Currents and Parameters. Rev. Educar, 14-15 (1988-89) 81-92.

108. Tusquets, J. (1969). Theory and practice of Comparative Pedagogy. Madrid: Spanish Teaching.

109. Vera M. Candau (1987). The Didactics in question. Madrid: Narcea Editions.

110. Virginia Martín A. (2007). The epistemological status and the object of the science of education. Doctoral thesis defended and approved at the University of Chile. San Juan - Argentina: Editorial of the Faculty of Philosophy, Humanities and Arts.

111. Wilhelm Dilthey (1965). Fundamentals of a pedagogy system. Buenos Aires: Ed. Losada.

112. Zabalza Beraza Miguel A. (2007).University Didactics. Rev. Bordón 59 (2-3), 2007, 489-509, ISSN: 0210-5934.

113. Zaballos Josefa (2010). Eduction, object of scientific reflection. Topic 5 of the Programming of the Subject of the Diploma in Teaching Specialty Early Childhood Education. CES Don Bosco: Teaching Studies. Taken from thehttp://www.cesdonbosco.com/profes/jzaballos. accessed June 23, 2012.

114. Zeitler Tomás E. (2010). The pedagogy of modernity. An approach to the forms and contents of teaching in Comenius, the Jesuits, the La Salle brothers and the Protestant Reformation. Faculty of Humanities, National University of the Northeast, Argentina. Ibero-American Journal of Education. No. 52/7 – 06/10/10. ISSN: 1681-5653.

115. Zuluaga, OL (1987). Pedagogy and History. Bogotá: National Forum Editions for Colombia.